OWN IT

8 Simple Secrets of Product Owner Success

Publisher: BoD – Books on Demand, Helsinki, Finland
Printer: BoD – Books on Demand, Norderstedt, Germany

ISBN: 978-952-800-619-0

Table of Contents

Foreword

When Arto told me about his new book and asked me to both review it and to write a foreword, I was both flattered and scared. I was flattered by Arto's trust in me and scared of writing this foreword. I wasn't scared about reviewing the book, as over the years we've worked jointly on several product manuals, guides, and white papers, in which Arto did the bulk of the writing and I then "polished" them (a bit).

Arto is one of the most humane tech leaders and educators that I've ever met, and it was a great pleasure to read and review this book (several revisions of it, as a matter of fact); it's a clear demonstration of his humanism, passion, and vast expertise in software development processes and best practices.

For this book, Arto has invested a lot of thought in putting forth a structure that makes his views and ideas approachable and easy to remember and use. The book was a pleasure to read and reminded me of more than a few "challenges" we've tackled (or just experienced) together, and I wish I had realized years ago some of the things I learned while reviewing the book.

This book should be read by every Product Owner, Product Manager, Project Manager, R&D Manager, Quality Assurance Manager, Scrum Master, Tech Lead . . . and every technology company founder and CEO. It helps those who need the skills and tools that this book teaches, but it also provides great insight to those stakeholders who need to understand why a software product development organization does (or at least should) work the way that Arto describes.

This book also contains novel concepts and ideas that will make the process more effective and enjoyable for product organizations that adopt them, and make the end products better for it.

—Petri Bäckström (who has served in numerous specialist, generalist and management roles in almost as many companies)

About the Author

Arto Kiiskinen has worked for over 20 years in product development, in different roles such as R&D Project Manager, Program Manager, Product Owner, Scrum Master, Test Engineer, R&D Team Lead, R&D Manager, and R&D Director. He has over 10 years of experience on agile methods, Scrum, Kanban, and experience on leading complex R&D projects that span multiple cultures, countries, and across large time zone differences.

He worked 15 years in Nokia, in different product and service areas such as mobile phone software development, digital service business and venture programs, and others. After his Nokia career, he has led the R&D organization in a smaller software company for 5 years.

As a trainer and coach, Arto has helped small and large companies and projects and programs of widely different industries transition to more effective and agile ways of working. Speeding up the path to reduced waste, increased efficiency, and superior team-learning and morale are Arto's main strengths and passions.

Arto is a PSM certified Scrum Master, PSPO certified Product Owner, certified ISTQB Tester, and certified SAFe Agilist. He has a Master's degree from Lappeenranta University of Technology.

He is the inventor or co-inventor in 15 U.S. patents and 6 EU patents.

Arto lives in Kirkkonummi, Finland with his wife, cat, and fleet of motorized and pedal powered vehicles.

https://www.linkedin.com/in/arto-kiiskinen-a98611/

Introduction

Product Owner Is the Most Important Role in Agile

Most organizations that are involved in research and development of new products or services acknowledge that one of their key success factors is R&D, especially the people who work in R&D. In modern R&D, almost everyone has access to same technologies and computer resources, but the people create the difference. People use their knowledge and skills and the organizations' resources and work together to create new, innovative products and services. R&D people with good motivation, tools, ways of working, freedom to self-organize, and vision are vitally important to any organization's future aspirations.

How does the organization maximize the value they get from their people? The answer is simple – in addition to having the correct skills, tools, and resources, the people need a clear vision and goals, work that's clearly specified and tested to be of the highest value in any given moment. In essence, that's what product ownership is all about.

The Product Owner is one of the principal roles in Agile, the others being the development team and the Scrum Master. While scrum is the most popular agile framework, even if the organization or team is using some other agile method, such as Kanban, most of the time, it still makes sense for them to have the roles of team, Scrum Master, and Product Owner. Sometimes, especially in smaller teams, a single person has multiple roles. This doesn't detract from the importance of still having the roles of Product Owner and Scrum Master in the team.

Having a Product Owner isn't mandatory. It's not a law. Some organizations don't have dedicated Product Owners in their R&D, yet they manage to create products of value. When we later on in the book discuss the concept of Product Owner, the tasks, routines, the Success Factors, and, eventually, the 8 Principles for Successful Product Owners, it doesn't mean that a single person always has to fill this role. The mission of this book is to describe to the reader what Product Ownership is, why the things that Product Owners do are important, and how one can be successful in the role of Product Owner. It would be best if the organization would endorse product ownership, but even if it doesn't, if someone does the same work, it will lead to good results.

Why is product ownership so important? It's because even the best teams need direction, and even the best self-organized teams benefit from having somebody with the single responsibility to define priorities. Product ownership doesn't mean product dictatorship – the main skills for a successful Product Owner is being able to communicate and listen to a lot of different voices, and then to boldly make informed and transparently communicated decisions.

The role of Product Owner is a challenge. But it's also a role in which you'll get satisfaction from optimizing the team performance and defining what gets done. You're part of creation of new things and new customer value. It feels good. And getting better at this role and achieving more success is fun. The mission of this book is to help you understand the why, what, and how of achieving more success as a Product Owner.

Who This Book Is Meant For

This book is targeted to help people who have a Product Owner role in their organization. It doesn't matter whether they're new or experienced. While it's recommended to read the whole book, an experienced Product Owner could dive directly into the 8 Principles in Part 3.

When starting as a Product Owner, it's important to understand the different responsibilities and routines of the role. For a person new to the job, it's advisable to read the entire book. This way, the reader can have some background on the execution of the tasks before proceeding to the mindset, values, and the 8 Principles.

In many organizations, the role of the Product Owner is poorly defined. In many cases, the responsibilities are divided between different people such as Product Manager, Scrum Master, Technical Lead, Architect, or Line Manager. In such a situation, this book can be used as a source of knowledge on agreeing who does what. One of the challenges for organizations is finding the correct person with the right skills who is still close-by and available to act as the Product Owner for the team.

While the book is targeted for Product Owners, people who work in Scrum Master, R&D Manager, or Product Manager roles might also benefit in understanding the methods behind successful product ownership.

About the Structure of The Book

The book consists of three parts:

* Part 1: Introduction to Product Ownership
* Part 2: The Success Factors for Product Owners
* Part 3: The 8 Principles for Successful Product Owners

To lay the foundation for the reader, Part 1 introduces why Product Owners are needed, how the role compares to other management roles, and what kind of routines and tasks Product Owners need to perform. This part of the book can be seen as the *why* for Product Owners.

In Part 2 we will look at the success factors for Product Owners. The success factors can be seen to define the *what* for Product Owners. Part 2 will start to reveal the concept of the Product Owner's Wheel of Success to the reader with its major success factors and subfactors.

The 8 Principles that are then introduced in Part 3 build on the success factors and help the reader understand the effective ways that they can work in the Product Owner role. The Principles define the *how* for Product Owners. The 8 Principles complete the Product Owner's Wheel of Success.

The book doesn't introduce details of Scrum or Kanban. The reader is assumed to know the basics of Scrum before proceeding. For a good and free introduction into Scrum, the reader can, for example, look at the Introduction to Scrum[1] webinar. Another good resource is The Scrum Guide[2]. Terms that are used in this book are explained there.

Many books have been written about product ownership. Similarly, there are lots of training courses for people new to the Product Owner role. The mission of this book isn't to be a comprehensive, detailed guide to the role. Rather, the book aims to offer an overview into the responsibilities and routines that each Product Owner will face, as well as offering a structure to the factors that affect whether or not a Product Owner is successful.

This book isn't the only book that offers useful knowledge to the aspiring Product Owner. In the course of reading the book, some very good additional readings will be listed in the text and in the footnotes. The recommended reading chapter at the end of the book collects these resources into a single list.

1   https://www.scrum.org/resources/introduction-scrum
2   https://www.scrum.org/resources/scrum-guide

Original Concepts

The following concepts introduced in this book were developed by the author and introduced for the first time in this book:

- *The Success Factors for Product Owners* (introduced in Part 2 of the book)
- *The 8 Principles for Successful Product Owners* (introduced in Part 3 of the book)
- *The Product Owner's Wheel of Success* (complete Wheel of Success is introduced first in the beginning of Part 3)
- *The DEEP Method for User Stories* (introduced in Part 1 – On User Stories)
- *The Backlog Swimming Pool* (introduced in Part 1 – On User Stories)
- *The Small Discussions Ceremony* (introduced in Part 3 – Principle #4)

Part 1

The Product Owner

Why Do Product Owners Exist?

A Product Owner's mission is to maximize the value generated by the product development team. This sounds easy, but in real life, it's a very difficult task. Maximizing the value means that the Product Owner has to find out the needs and requirements of multiple stakeholders, balance and value them, and then make sure that they're documented clearly and communicated effectively to the development teams.

This means that in addition to the development team, the Product Owner has to communicate with multiple different parties inside and outside the organization, such as other Product Owners and Project Managers in the product development organization, company sales department, marketing, product management, the company management, operations, customer support, customers and third parties and partners. The Product Owner must understand all the different requests and requirements and customer problems, and then manage this complex situation to arrive to a prioritized list of things for the development team to investigate, design, implement and release.

You can already see from this that a lot of the Product Owner's work is communication, seeking understanding, testing ideas, defining of details and cooperation with others. But it should also be about actively reject-

Product Owners exist to maximize the value of development work.

ing ideas, because there will always be many more ideas and requests coming in than the development team can work on with reasonable quality.

If all the feedback, communication, and ideas are allowed to freely flow to the development team, it leads to frequent interruptions, task-switching, inability to focus, poor prioritization, and inevitably – as a result – poor quality and low team morale. Product Owners exist to manage this inflow of ideas to the development team, and their success is measured by how well the team can deliver what the customers want, deliver value with least amount of task switching and interruptions, and have good team morale.

Product Owner Decides What the Team Works On

The whole point of the role of Product Owner is being someone who makes informed decisions regarding what is the highest priority item at any given time. The development team has a limited capacity, and any work they start will quickly become an expensive investment as the hours start to pile up. The Product Owner's job is to make sure that the investment is put to the best possible use.

The Product Owner does this by limiting the input of the rest of the organization to the development team. She rejects ideas or feedback that aren't valuable and allows only items of sufficient value to reach the team. She also maximizes the value that the team produces. She does this by maintaining a prioritized list of items, called the product backlog.

The team always knows that when they want to start new work, they can take an item from the top of the backlog, and it will be the most valuable thing that the team can start at any given time. When using Scrum, the team knows that selecting items to the sprint from the top of the backlog delivers most value and are ready for the actual development to start.

Similarly, the Product Owner and the team collaborate on the items on the backlog, making them more detailed, accurate, and valuable. This is achieved in workshops and discussions where the team and the Product Owner work on the backlog items together. Sometimes, the items are too large, and they're split into smaller items. Sometimes, the items require studies to find out the technical feasibility or usability of the items. Sometimes, the Product Owner may choose to work with Product Management to make sure that the business feasibility of any given idea is confirmed well enough that it makes sense to invest development team time on it.

95% of the Product Owner role is communication, collaboration and discussions.

It's important to remember that ideas almost always don't hit the mark when they're introduced to the team. All development must be iterative. Product Owners must be aware of how much the idea has been tested and iterated before entering the team. If it's likely that certain assumptions must still be tested before final implementation, the Product Owner avoids investing the team's capacity to something that needs to be changed later. The Product Owner must make sure that the team is implementing the right thing.

What If There Would Be No Product Owner?

Without a Product Owner, the team would have a very difficult time guessing which request is most valuable. Often, the lack of a Product Owner will lead to many people shouting to the development team, and the person who shouts the loudest wins and gets their item into the development team sprint, until someone else shouts even louder! This kind of a situation is very stressful for the team and can also lead to task-switching, forcing the team members to work on multiple things at the same time. All this will lead to poor quality, a stressful work environment, and non-optimal value.

Product Owner and Product Manager

Why do we need Product Owners? Shouldn't the Product Manager take care of all the things that belong to the Product Owner? This is a statement that's often heard. It's very true that the job of Product

Manager, in principle, contains all of the tasks and responsibilities that the Product Owner should be doing. In this sense, it can be said that Product Owner is a role, and Product Manager is the job. While it's true that, especially in smaller organizations and startups, the Product Manager is perfectly positioned to act as the Product Owner, in other situations and in practice it can often be useful to have a dedicated Product Manager and a separate person working in the role of Product Owner.

While both the Product Manager and the Product Owner have the objective to choose and define the right things for the development team to work on, the role of Product Manager focuses much more on the *discovery* side, while Product Owner takes care of the

> *Product Manager focuses on Discovery. Product Owner takes care of efficient Delivery.*

gritty details of the actual solution *delivery*. A perfect person might be able to do the work of both, but how many of us are perfect?

As this book is about product ownership, we focus here more on delivery than discovery. While it's still extremely important that the team is iterating the solution also during the solution delivery, the prospective Product Owner should still remember that it's very costly to do large changes of direction while implementing the product. Therefore, as the Product Owner's responsibility is to maximize the value that the product teams generate, she must also think about discovery. Has the product concept or features that are now progressing from Product Manager to her area of responsibility been tested enough? The largest waste is generated when the product team, under guidance of the Product Owner, creates a solution that the market doesn't want or need, or that cannot be sold because of some business or legal reason. These kinds of situations can even be career-killing mistakes, and it's all too easy to point the finger at the Product Owner for these kinds of failures. To avoid spending expensive development team effort on work that aims to do the wrong thing, the Product Owner must cooperate with the Product Manager to study, test, and investigate the customer problem to get enough proof to make the involvement of the development team the logical next step. We will talk more about the different stages of iteration later.

One of the reasons a separate Product Owner can be useful is so that the Product Owner can be much closer to the development team or teams. One key success factor for the team is the accessibility and availability of the Product Owner to guide them during the development. Product Managers have much more tasks and wider range of responsibilities, so it's more difficult for them to work close enough to the development teams. Having an easily accessible Product Owner nearby acts like oil in the machinery, making things roll along smoother and faster and with less friction. It also allows effective adjustment of small details during implementation sprints.

Both the Product Owner and the Product Manager need to be experts about the product and the users, especially the problems that the users of the product have. But while the Product Manager needs to have some technical insight into the way the product is developed and built, the Product Owner can have deeper knowledge about the technology and how the development works through ways and processes. In this sense, the Product Owner can be seen as taking some load off the Product Manager's hands and making her life a bit easier. The Product Manager can then focus even more effort on the things that she will do much more than the Product Owner: testing and studying product features and ideas early on in

The Product Owner exists to help the Product Manager. Cooperation is the key to repeated success.

their lifecycle; talking to wide range of customers, end users, and stakeholders; understanding details of the business model that will dictate what and how things need to get built; and definition of the product vision and long-term roadmap.

It's very important that the Product Owner and the Product Manager have a good working relationship. With a good working relationship, they can agree on the division of work and responsibilities on a detailed level. Product Owners exist to help the Product Manager.

This said, knowing the details of Product Management is also recommended for people who work in the Product Owner role. An excellent book on this is Marty Cagan's *Inspired: How to Create Tech Products Customers Love*[3]. The book details perfectly the job and the long list of tasks and responsibilities of Product Managers (and at also leaves the reader wondering how on earth all those tasks can be done by one person). People working in a Product Owner role should read the book

---

3   Marty Cagan: Inspired: How to Create Tech Products Customers Love https://www.amazon.com/ INSPIRED-Create-Tech-Products-Customers-ebook/dp/B077NRB36N

with the mindset of choosing the things that they can help the Product Manager do. As with every large and complex job, if the Product Owner and Product Manager have a good working relationship and if they're able to divide the work and responsibilities effectively, they can achieve more and better results than just trusting a single, overworked, and soon-to-be burnt-out Product Manager to do the job.

This book and Mr. Cagan's book complement each other. Where Mr. Cagan's book describes well the tasks, the content, and the *what* of Product Management and as a subset of it, *Own It: 8 Simple Secrets for Product Owner Success* goes beyond the *what,* and describes the *ways of working* and the *how* that lead to repeated success in the Product Owner role.

What About Other Managers?

Scrum itself defines only three roles – The Product Owner, The Scrum Master, and the development team. However, in addition to the already discussed Product Manager, typical organizations have also other types of managers surrounding the R&D department and working with them:

- R&D Managers
- Project Managers
- Quality Assurance Managers / Testing Managers

How does the Product Owner (PO) role compare to these management positions? The first difference is that the PO isn't a line management role. Product Owners don't have subordinates. In fact, having subordinates is one of the common mistakes that we will talk about later.

While pure Scrum doesn't have testers, Testing Managers, or a QA Managers, it's still quite common to see these titles around development teams. This is fine; Scrum is a guideline more than a rigid set of rules. Organizations will find what works best for them. Still, the original spirit of a Scrum Product Owner is that she is ultimately the person who has decision power on the backlog items and responsibility for having the items clear and ready for the development team to consume. This responsibility over the backlog items and their priority is the core of Product Ownership. The Product Owner may delegate error screening to a QA Manager or an Error Manager, and she may delegate the writing of user stories to suitable persons, but she is still ultimately responsible.

The Challenge of Product Ownership

With an efficient and successful Product Owner, the team always works on the most important thing and is sure that the thing is also specified to necessary detail. The work is productive, fun, and the team is able to get a sense of accomplishment. As we see in the 8 Principles, a successful Product Owner also keeps the team informed, motivated, and continuously improving, allowing the team to learn and grow as well as achieve.

The role of the Product Owner is challenging, but it's also very rewarding. The required mindset and skills of a successful Product Owner are now compacted in this book into a set of concrete principles and the success factors that will help the reader to understand the role, how to succeed in it, and where to improve her own skills and capabilities.

The Routines

Working in the role of a Product Owner usually means that you'll be quite busy. There are constant questions, issues, errors, problems, investigations, and conflicts surfacing from many directions. One risk with this kind of a busy schedule at work is that the Product Owner works only on the issues that surface; she begins to work in reactive mode. Working in reactive mode, the Product Owner could be easily forget to do all the background tasks that are essential for success.

As we will see later in Part 2, achieving success requires getting good results in many different kinds of factors. Some of these factors (e.g., trying to decide which errors to fix to keep the release schedule), will prompt the Product Owner for action. However, some of the factors don't directly remind about themselves; for example, having enough customer interaction or stakeholder communication.

All-important tasks don't remind you about themselves.

To stay organized, the Product Owner should keep in mind the different regular routines that are useful in her work. In this chapter, we will investigate what kind of tasks are repeated daily, weekly, per sprint, or monthly.

Many of the routines listed next are Scrum ceremonies and, as such, can be facilitated by the Scrum Master. The Product Owner and the Scrum Master should agree on the practicalities of facilitating the sessions.

Daily Tasks

Here are some tasks that the Product Owner should do every day. Obviously, these four tasks aren't everything that the Product Owner does, but they typically repeat every day.

Checking the Backlog

One of the things that the successful Product Owner does every single day is making sure that the backlog is in good order.

Keeping the backlog in good order means that the top of the backlog is in exactly the correct prioritized order. This needs to be the instinct of the Product Owner. Whenever a new issue surfaces, or something is learned from the product or the environment or from an existing issue on the backlog, the first instinct of the successful Product Owner should be to think:

- Where does this issue go on the backlog?
- Does the introduction of this issue affect anything else on the backlog?

Without going too deep into the issue workflows, an essential part for helping the Product Owner do this initial issue prioritization is an issue workflow that assigns all new issues to a state that's easy for the Product Owner to notice; for example, "New." Then it's easy to set up a routine to check once or twice a day what new issues have been reported.

The Product Owner can look at the new issues and determine their initial place in the backlog. It's very likely that in further discussions with the team and stakeholders, this initial place in the priority order will change. As the understanding of the issue will grow during discussions, the issue is described in more detail and estimated, the issue state can be changed to reflect this.

The prioritization should extend beyond the time an item is started. Sometimes, an item's priority changes as work on it commences. Perhaps the developers discover that a larger problem is behind the initial problem description. This is very common – a seemingly innocent issue is selected for fixing, and once the developer uncovers the root cause, it's suddenly the explanation for a wide variety of recent or mysterious problems.

The Product Owner must have an instinct for prioritization; where does this new issue go on the backlog and how does it affect other issues?

Sometimes, an item's urgency changes while work on it is ongoing. An item was started without clear understanding of its deadline, but once it's underway, further communication with stakeholders will reveal that the item is actually quite urgent and serious. So, the Product Owner must remain vigilant for priority changes throughout the work on the item. The initial "before" priority isn't always the one that the item ends up with at the end of its journey through the team's process.

Error Screening

Screening errors is similar to the first routine of backlog item priority, but it goes a bit deeper – checking the error quality as well. Some Product Owners do this themselves, others have other people do the error screening, or do it together in a screening meeting. Delegating the error screening work to a QA Manager or Error Manager makes sense when the product is large and there are lots of errors. In smaller products, the Product Owner should be able to do the screening herself. However, since the errors or bugs are part of the backlog, it will always be ultimately the Product Owner's responsibility that they're clear and correctly prioritized.

If the screening is set up as a meeting, it should happen at least twice a week. If the Product Owner screens the errors herself, it should be done at least once every day.

The screening means that the error is reviewed for:

1. Correct severity (fatal, critical, major, minor).
2. Instant decision is made to keep it alive or reject.

3. The title is checked for clarity.
4. The error description is checked for clear steps and good actual vs. desired behavior.
5. The "more info" section of the error is checked for info on reproducibility and negative scenarios – when the error cannot be reproduced or how user can recover from it.

All the above will give the Product Owner a sense of priority for the error. Quite often, the error needs to be clarified further before it's of sufficient quality. Also, a very good practice is to have a different state in the workflow for unscreened vs. screened errors. This allows the team to see if the Product Owner has approved the error description and severity.

When time, environment, and the Product Owner's skills allow, a very good practice is to attempt to reproduce the error yourself. You'll soon develop an instinct on when this is needed, but it especially is helpful when the error reproducing steps are unclear. When you can attempt to reproduce the error with the steps or description in the original description, then you can add information and value to the error report.

Attempting to reproduce errors will give you invaluable hands-on feel on the use of the product – just make sure that it doesn't take too much of your time!

If the error cannot be reproduced with the initial error description from the originator, rather than starting a ping-pong game of assigning the error back to originator, the Product Owner or someone else from the team can try different ways to reproduce the error. Bouncing errors back and worth should be avoided because it consumes time and usually irritates the originator.

Another thing that should be avoided is assigning an unreproducible error to developers. Although, it's very useful to get developer's insight on a difficult to reproduce bug. The team should figure out who is best positioned from skills, environment access, and workload to attempt to clarify an unclear error.

The investigation of errors is something that the Product Owner can do in a limited fashion. Doing so will educate the Product Owner on the product features and the problems. It will also give good insight on end user's problems and frustrations and enable you to prioritize better.

If you decide to participate in the error clarification yourself, and attempt to reproduce errors while screening them, you must have a sense of how much time this takes from your other responsibilities as Product Owner. Spend enough time so that you're certain that you have a good enough competence on the product and a good understanding of the current error inflow, but no more. If you can educate the organization to produce good quality errors then the error clarification will require less focus.

Communication with The Team

The Product Owner should have a daily routine to have a chat with the team. It's recommended for the Product Owner to participate in the team's daily standup meeting. She will hear how work on the items is progressing and if there are any difficulties or unclear issues. She will also have a perfect opportunity to share any important piece of information with the team. Having this kind of routine will lower any communication barriers or thresholds for asking questions. It will also promote instant sharing of any information to the complete team. It's usually best to check errors and the backlog first and have the team communication session afterwards.

Walk to Chat with a Stakeholder

After the Product Owner has a clear understanding on the latest status with errors and the backlog and has a good situational awareness of the currently ongoing tasks from the team communication session, she is ready to proceed to other work that she needs to do that day. One of the things she should try to do every day is check up on some of the product's stakeholders.

The list of stakeholders that a project has is usually long: sales, marketing, product management, company management, customer support, operations, logistics, pilot customers, etc. As with team communication, the goal should be to establish good communication with the stakeholders so that any important piece of information that affects the product or the project is immediately noticed and communicated

Walking around and talking to people will lower the communication threshold and reduce the chance of surprises.

throughout the stakeholder network. This way, the threshold for sharing information remains low. In addition, the people must be given ample opportunities to communicate with you.

One way achieving the above works extremely well is just walking to people and having a chat. Instead of reports or weekly meetings, an informal chat will offer you a chance to share the status and get the other party to react to the news and ask questions.

A common way to try to handle the stakeholder communication is to hold a weekly "update meeting" or a "status meeting" with a presentation by either the Product Owner or the Product Manager. This will almost always yield worse results than one-to-one discussions. People want different information from the status of the development: a salesperson might want to know her favorite feature's status or position on the backlog or even to see or try a prototype or a demo. The CEO might want to know the overall progress toward a release deadline. Customer support might want to know if the team can have capacity to help them investigate some customer issues. Everybody wants different information – so serve them individually.

With individual chats, you can also get an honest, undiluted opinion and answers from the stakeholder on their needs. People are usually more hesitant to open their mouths in a meeting. A lunch is one way to do these face-to-face sessions, but don't forget that the Product Owner should also have time for lunch with the development team at least once or twice a week.

In addition to the potential "stakeholder-lunches," a successful Product Owner walks around. She can walk to the Product Manager's office, or the sales team office, or customer support, or the company CEO, and if the other person seems available for a quick chat, have that chat. You can (and probably should) have some news or information to share with them to not be a time thief. Offer something of value for them – some piece of information – and you'll get something of value back. The point of the chat isn't to be a long discussion or a meeting – it can only take couple minutes. The point is to establish frequent communication paths and opportunities for stakeholders to express their wishes and needs to you. If you do this kind of impromptu visits, the other stakeholders are also more likely to visit you and have a lower threshold to come to you with important information. This all increases the communication efficiency of the organization.

The Order of Daily Tasks

The logical order for the daily tasks is:

- Check the errors
- Check the backlog
- Talk to the team
- Talk to a stakeholder

This order makes sense because error situations can require urgent reactions, and, in any case, serious errors are always more important than anything on the backlog. Then, to be able to listen and react to the team daily, it pays to be up-to-date on what's next on the backlog. If the next item on the backlog requires work for it to be ready, then you can plan for it. Finally, after checking errors and the backlog and talking to the team, you're ready to talk to a stakeholder, comfortable in the knowledge that you have the absolutely latest information on the product development fresh in your mind.

The daily tasks can be shown as in Figure 1:

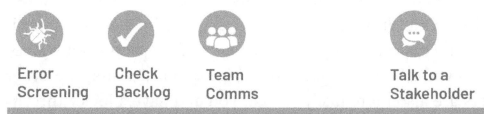

Figure 1 Daily Tasks

Weekly Tasks

The following tasks are the most important tasks that repeat every week.

Backlog Grooming

The most important ceremony that should be repeated every week is the common backlog grooming session (sometimes also called the backlog refinement session). Typically, the session should be timeboxed to take an hour, but at various stages of the project, it's likely that more time may need to be invested to keep the understanding of the work ahead at a suitable level.

The grooming session can be used to work on the items that are likely to make it to the next Scrum sprint, but its real target is to work on the items that go beyond the next sprint. Preferably, the team can use the grooming session to discuss and add detail to items for the next three to five sprints. Going beyond that starts to push the detailed planning too far into the future. Doing detailed plans too far into the future can result in wasted effort, because things change in the details, and people also forget things easily. If you would specify details for an item that will only be started 3–4 months into the future, you need to spend much more time to document the details very clearly in order for them to be understandable quickly later.

At some point, the Product Owner may decide to expand the grooming session to be more like a story-writing workshop. This makes sense when there's a higher than average inflow of new ideas, such as in starting phases of a new release or project. In the workshop, the team can write the stories together or in small groups or pairs. The work could be assisted by the user story mapping method.

The grooming can proceed with the Scrum Master or Product Owner pulling the individual backlog items up on the shared screen where everybody can see them, and then the team can discuss the detailed description of the story. The progress of the discussion should be documented. One good and efficient way to document the discussion is to almost instantly write everything the team members say into "bullet points" that add and expand the original description of the backlog item. The important part is to keep logging the discussed items so that everyone can see them (and, therefore, agree to or disagree on them) as the secretary writes them down.

In addition to adding details, the grooming session can also be used to do effort estimation. The most common way to do this is to use story points. A small story is one point, and then the team uses this as a reference to estimate whether other stories are bigger. Are they two or five times bigger? Or 10

> *Backlog grooming / refinement session is the most important regular weekly meeting for a Product Owner.*

times? The team should set a maximum size limit for stories that are at the top of the backlog, ready to be started in the sprint. This limit should be decided and adjusted in the team retrospectives. If a team finds delivering planned content in sprints challenging, one of the first things to adjust would be to make this story maximum size limit smaller, forcing the team to split stories.

One caveat with estimation is that it's usually easy to ask the estimate from the most "senior" members of the team. The problem with this is that these people also tend to do the work the fastest and, therefore, give lower effort estimates. Planning poker[4] is a method that's designed to avoid this; it forces more people to give an estimate and then discuss the differences in estimates. You could also use other methods to arrive at an effort estimate.

Effort estimation isn't meant to be totally accurate. It doesn't really matter if a story is two story points or five. What matters is the discussion,

---

4   https://en.wikipedia.org/wiki/Planning_poker

adding the detail into the stories, and identifying stories that are clearly too large and should be split.

Splitting stories, while perhaps initially difficult, is an important team-skill. There are multiple approaches to splitting stories. One of the founders of the Scrum Alliance, Mike Cohn[5] advocates the use of the "SPIDR[6]" method (Spikes, Paths, Interfaces, Data, Rules). With SPIDR, the team can think, for example, what data or what interfaces the complete story would implement, and then split the implementation to two or more separate stories. A smaller story is easier to implement and verify with good quality. Another way to split stories is to identify the elements, the building blocks in a story, and then think of the simplest possible way to implement something from each element.

Grooming with Large Teams

Larger teams (approaching 10 or so members) can choose not to groom with the whole team. This allows the team to work more efficiently, but the risk with this approach is that information isn't shared equally among team members. For example, it's easy to forget to involve testers enough,

In estimating stories, the exact size isn't important. What's important is identifying stories that are too big or unclear and should be described and discussed more and split into smaller stories.

5   https://www.mountaingoatsoftware.com/company/about-mike-cohn
6   https://www.mountaingoatsoftware.com/exclusive/spidr-poster-download

leading to user stories that contain insufficient details on how they will be tested. If this kind of grooming practice is in use, special care should be taken to share story content to the whole team after the details have been added. This could be done in the actual sprint planning session.

The grooming session is an extremely important session for the team's performance. While the session itself can be short, only an hour per week, it might require considerable time and effort in preparation and also in follow up actions. The Product Owner and the team should not underestimate the impact well-specified backlog items have on the results. One of the most common problems in agile teams is that the backlog items aren't specified well enough or discussed thoroughly enough in common sessions. Focus and effort in the grooming session is a good investment.

Coordinate With Other Teams

When a project consists of multiple scrum teams (and sometimes also multiple Product Owners), it's necessary to coordinate the progress of each team every week. This is usually the task of Scrum Masters, and the ceremony is called Scrum-of-Scrums (SoS). The SoS should be a synchronization and feedback loop for a multiteam program as the daily scrum meeting is for a single team. While the SoS is facilitated and run by Scrum Masters, it's good for the Product Owners to participate in this meeting.

The meeting should run through all the teams that participate in the project, and within a few minutes, give a status report on items that are of interest to the other teams: dependency issues, merging and integration issues, learnings and plans on items that might interest others. Each team's turn to speak should be used to offer opportunity for a quick question or two. At the end, the confidence level of participants on the targets of the current and next sprints or the overall release schedule can be checked with a simple show of hands.

The Order of Weekly Tasks

Weekly tasks can be summed up in a picture as shown in Figure 2.

Figure 2 Weekly tasks

Every Sprint

These are the most important tasks that repeat every sprint. For teams that use Kanban, these tasks could still repeat regularly, every 2–4 weeks. Obviously, Kanban doesn't have sprints as such, but, typically, even teams using Kanban will benefit in some form of planning for the future.

Sprint Planning

Sprint planning is the most important routine for the Product Owner. When preparing for it, the Product Owner thinks about what her wishes for the contents for the next sprint are, and she then brings this proposal to the planning meeting.

The targets for the meeting are:

- to make sure that the most important items are selected to the sprint backlog,
- make a final check that the team understands the items adequately,
- verify that the items selected for the sprint are described in detail, and
- get a commitment from the team that the items should be doable in the next sprint.

Getting a commitment from the team for "this is doable" is important for teams that are new to agile or Scrum. When the team's use of Scrum has matured, it can relax the emphasis on commitment and switch to do targeted content rather than committed content. The team should use the velocity of last few sprints as a guide on how much work to load into the sprint.

Sprint planning is the final chance for making sure that each item on the sprint backlog is well described (in writing!) and discussed face-to-face with the team. It would be best that the descriptions were done beforehand in the backlog grooming or the sprint pre-planning sessions, but if they have not been done, they must be done now. In no circumstances should a team allow items without any description or details on the Sprint backlog.

One further thing that should be observed in the sprint planning session is that the team doesn't select or try to commit to deliver too large stories. Teams must have an upper effort limit on the stories that they select. It's very common that during the discussion and while adding the details to the story, the team notices that the effort will be higher than the agreed maximum limit. In this situation, the team should split the story to two or more stories.

The effort limit is very important because without an effort limit, the team can start any size story. Too large stories have a very high likelihood of not being finished in the sprint. Large stories also inevitably aren't described as well as smaller stories, and usually result in more errors and lower quality.

Preplanning

Preplanning is a routine that's optional. It's basically a short "heads-up" meeting that reveals what the Product Owner is currently thinking for the next sprint content. Its purpose is to allow team to react on items that require some further individual analysis or studies. Sometimes, it's needed for individuals to look at existing code before they can estimate

The sprint preplanning ceremony reduces surprises and allows better preparation for the actual planning session, making it shorter, smoother, and more productive.

the effort. With a preplanning meeting, they can "borrow" some time from the previous sprint to prepare for the sprint planning. Preplanning speeds up the actual sprint planning session because there is less uncertainty in estimating how complex the tasks will be, and the people will be more familiar with the content.

Preplanning should be held 2 to 3 days before the sprint end. It usually is a short meeting and should result in some individual investigative work.

Sprint Review and Demo

The Product Owner must take part in the sprint's end review and demo session. She must approve the sprint deliverables and the potential sprint release, as well as selectively challenge the team on whether the definition of done was followed. On the other hand, the end of the sprint is a perfect opportunity to acknowledge progress and give positive feedback and encouragement for the team and individuals on the things that were done right and the team's achievements.

The sprint-end demo is also often a place to have other stakeholders visit to get a view on the state of the product or service. The Product Owner is usually the person to coordinate such visits and let the team know if a visitor is joining the demo session. The feedback from such visitors is very valuable and any demo session should cater and expect comments and questions from the audience.

It's important to understand that the Sprint Review is for the team to reflect on how this sprint went, and the Demo is for the team to show to stakeholders and other teams what was achieved. The audiences are quite different, so, most of the time, it makes sense to have these sessions separately, and not as a one long "review and demo" meeting.

Stakeholder Update

In addition to updating the stakeholders in the sprint demo, the Product Owner should also have a regular "newsletter" update going out to anybody willing to listen. The contents of the newsletter could be:

1. What has been released in the past 2 weeks
2. What will be released next
3. Specifics on latest important features developed in the team or for the product (with screenshots)
4. Highest severity issues currently under investigation (with workarounds or an estimate when they will be addressed and when the fix will be released).
5. Any other interesting topics
6. Call to action – usually asking for comments, questions or feedback

The Product Owner should welcome feedback, comments or questions to the newsletter. Keeping the newsletter as visual and concise as possible works better than a long and wordy email.

Make your newsletter valuable to readers with a quick-to-read initial executive summary as well as screenshots and images of new features. Invite feedback!

Pre-Development and Testing of Backlog Items

Some items require pre-development. This can mean user interface work, specification writing or technical or usability studies. The need for such work should be identified latest in the backlog grooming or sprint pre-planning sessions, and it's usually up to the Product Owner to coordinate the pre-development work.

A considerable amount of the pre-development should be investigations and testing of potential features or ideas for the product. This needs to be tightly coordinated with the Product Manager, because it's usually the Product Manager who drives this early feature and idea screening and development process. The idea is to study and investigate many more ideas than actually can be implemented, and then allow only the ones that show most promise to proceed to the product backlog. It's very important that the Product Owner and some developers or designers from the development team participate this early idea screening. If the organization learns to use prototypes and the early testing of ideas efficiently, the changes in implementation will usually be much more focused on small details, and larger "pivot" style changes of direction are rarely needed when the actual final implementation is done in the development team.

Typically, organizations don't test enough ideas. Marty Cagan's book mentioned earlier is recommended reading on this subject.

The Order of Tasks in Sprints

The per-sprint repeating tasks could be located on the timeline as shown in the Figure 3.

| Sprint Planning | Stakeholder update | Backlog item Pre-devt | Pre Planning | Review & Demo |

| DAY 1 | DAY 2 | DAY 3 | DAY 4 | DAY 5 | DAY 1 | DAY 2 | DAY 3 | DAY 4 | DAY 5 |

Figure 3 Per-sprint tasks

Monthly

Retrospectives

One of the key things that the development teams should do regularly is retrospectives. They should be held either every sprint, or, alternatively, every month. Teams that are new to Scrum, or that have just started working together, should do retrospectives more often, every two weeks or every sprint. More mature teams or teams that use Kanban, can do retrospectives monthly.

Although the Product Owner isn't facilitating the retrospectives for the team, she must follow up on the team retros. First, she should make sure that the team is keeping them. Second, she should participate in them to offer her feedback. Third, she should make sure that the team is effectively implementing improvements and isn't getting bogged down in a boring or unproductive retrospective format. Thus, the team and the Scrum Master are responsible for the retrospectives, and when the Product Owner participates, she does so in the role of a team member, not in the role of Product Owner.

We will talk more about retrospectives and learning later in the book in Part 3.

Customer Contacts and Discussions

In the day-to-day grind, it's very easy for the Product Owner to forget to nurse deeper relationships with customers. The Product Owner's ability to prioritize and get "fast idea-spin" feedback would improve if she had direct channels to some selected customers. Having a *"customer best friend"* is important.

The customer best friend means that the Product Owner has a very close relationship with one or more customers. The relationship is such that the Product Owner feels that she can call or email the customer about almost any issue as a quick, low-overhead way to get feedback. The added knowledge of such market insight is invaluable.

Customer Best Friend can be your reference customer. They're invaluable in providing feedback and also assisting sales activities

How does one then get such "customer best friends"? This questions is best solved together with Product

Management. You should find out what customer groups are most important and highest potential for your product right now, and then figure out which customers would be interested to offer feedback for the R&D team. Not all customers are willing to spend time reviewing demos, plans or prereleases of new software. You have to find the correct customers and then make sure that you have the correct customer contact person. You should then show and prove to the customer contact person why it will be beneficial and valuable for her to work with you. Having access to early prereleases gives the customer visibility on upcoming features, and an opportunity to affect the development.

Developing the relationship to the "friendship" stage takes time and you must remember to keep regular contact. Before you reach the level where the relationship with the customer contact rests on a solid base, you should consciously think that each contact and question offers her value – either an opportunity to express her wishes about the product or information on problematic situations in the field, information on progress on issues that she has previously reported, or information on upcoming new features that you know might affect her business.

Sometimes, it's a good idea to invite the customer to review a demo in the R&D office; other times, the demo can be taken to her office. Occasionally, it might also be a good idea to have a longer meeting off-site with some more people to make the cooperation deeper and to spread the knowledge of the product in the customer's organization.

Common Mistakes

When learning about something, it's always good to look at what not to do – what mistakes you should try to avoid. Thus, in this chapter, let's look at the most common mistakes for Product Owners.

No Discussion With Team

Perhaps the biggest mistake that a Product Owner can make is to not be available for the team to discuss the backlog items.

As we saw in the routines section, discussion about the backlog items is crucial to achieving success. Discussion is the only effective way to spread understanding about the backlog item to multiple developers and testers in the team. Spreading the understanding allows the team to assign the task dynamically to anyone and also allows better quality peer reviews or pair programming, and higher quality testing. Effort estimation after discussion is more accurate, resulting in fewer sprint overflows. Finally, through discussion, the specification of the backlog item is usually made more accurate and the number of errors is reduced.

Not discussing the backlog items with your team face-to-face is the biggest mistake the Product Owner can make!

There are so many benefits in the discussion of each backlog item, that it's simply unbelievable how often one encounters organizations who don't do this discussion regularly and methodically. Backlog grooming and sprint planning sessions are ceremonies that facilitate the discussion, but it doesn't need to end there. In fact, ad-hoc type discussion on individual backlog items is also recommended.

If the Product Owner doesn't offer the team the possibility to discuss the backlog items, she is risking that they implement the wrong thing, which is the most waste that you can have in an agile R&D.

Having No Direct Customer Contact

The Product Owner has to have direct customer contacts! Her main responsibility is to prioritize the work and make sure that the backlog items are valuable and that the team delivers maximum value. This is *impossible* without detailed and fresh understanding of customer problems that the product is trying to solve.

One problem that many Product Owners face is that they're very busy, and the day-to-day work that's related to the delivery of already planned functionality takes so much of their time, that they find it very difficult to maintain customer relationships that would allow them to visit customers or be in contact with them in other ways. The other problems that can result in too little customer contacts are that the organization can have some sort of policy or protectionism of who can actually be talking to the customers.

The "customer best friends" or reference customers that we discussed earlier is a way to maintain a deep and meaningful relationship with selected customers. You should not have too many of these, and they could be split with the Product Manager. The Product Manager cab handle a few customers and the Product Owner a few more. The reference customers can change from one release to the next, or from one market entry to the next. The main thing is that they exist and are actively involved in the development of features from idea to final implementation.

Agile Waterfalling

Everybody laughs at the old ways of doing software development. Waterfall, spending months or years collecting requirements, then months or years in design, implementation and then finally integration and testing, is so 1990s, right? Nobody in their right mind does things this way anymore.

Not so fast, cowboy! How often do you encounter a situation that some product idea or a feature progresses to the development team backlog with only a vague idea about the business case or customer need? How often does it happen that the Product Owner and the development team are asked to develop a feature and they're unsure of the actual reason why this feature is needed? How often does it happen that the information around the feature request or product idea is unclear enough that the team and the Product Owner struggle to even write detailed user stories or add acceptance criteria to them? How often does it happen that the team starts working to develop a solution and then learns something profound during the implementation and has to dramatically change the concept to meet the actual need of the customers? How often does it happen that the team develops features that turn out not to be so popular when launched? Does this sound more familiar? The team is being as agile as it can, but when the ideas it's getting from the discovery process aren't being tested iteratively before they arrive, it's only able to get small gains by being iterative during the implementation. You're trying to be agile in a barrel that's still going toward the waterfall.

The best Product Owners recognize this and work with the Product Manager to investigate items that require testing before they're taken into the backlog. Sometimes, this can mean technical feasibility or usability studies with quickly developed prototypes or even a paper mockup from a designer. Sometimes, other factors, such as the business model, pricing model, or legal implications, need to be investigated in some other way. Whatever is needed, it's far better to study these issues upstream of the actual development process, and the Product Owner is responsible for preventing ideas that haven't been studied enough to enter the implementation process.

Blindly Adding More Features

The next pitfall for Product Owners is to just blindly keep adding all possible features to the product. If you think that the more "bullet points" the new version spec sheet has, the more likely customers will purchase it, you have missed the point completely. The Product Owner's job is to add the most valuable features, not the maximum number of features.

If the Product Owner always only keeps on adding more and more features, just based on what can be done, there is a danger that priorities are based on what is possible to do, not what is most valuable for the company and the customers. It's also possible that no general theme or analysis of the usage of current features is done. This can lead to products that have too many features and are confusing to use and difficult to test and maintain.

Understanding what is valuable and what isn't is usually done with close cooperation with product management. Value can mean more than just monetary value. Sometimes, the knowledge value of implementing something new is also high enough that this kind of features can be added to the product. Another way to look at this is reduced cost. Sometimes, features reduce costs for your company or your customers, allowing you to charge higher prices or increase your own profit margin.

Generally, Product Managers have the main responsibility to think about value in features, but Product Owners need to be aware of this, and cooperate

Customers have problems – we come up with the innovative solutions!

closely with Product Managers. One final thought on this is that, sometimes, it pays to group features together when they're clearly from the same topic area. This might make marketing communications of the new release easier for customers to understand. When customers realize that all the features of a given topic area are in the new release, it might be enough to sway them to make the purchase decision. In this situation, even lower value features might rise in priority if they're seen as complementing some other higher value feature of the same topic area.

An important thing is also to remember that customers should not specify the features. Customers certainly have problems or needs, and we need to have a very good understanding of these. But our customers should not tell us what we should do. Customers have problems, and we must own and deliver the innovations to solve those problems. In the same way, it's much better if Product Management and also the Product Owner understand and detail the customer problem for the engineers, and spend less time in specifying the solution. Engineers are usually very good in coming up with solutions to clearly stated problems.

Never Saying No to Anything

Another mistake is when the Product Owner acts as a "backlog secretary," meaning that she just blindly writes everything to the backlog. Even if she attempts to keep the items in prioritized order, this leads very quickly to the backlog growing beyond all capabilities of the development team to build in reasonable time.

The biggest lie of Product Owners is: *"I will add it to the backlog."* This tells the person who made the request that her idea was logged down (perhaps it was a good idea and perhaps the team is implementing it soon).

The Product Owner's biggest (and most common) lie: "I will add it to the backlog."

But for anyone who has worked in R&D, the statement is understood differently. It means that it's put at the bottom of the backlog where it might remain forever, gathering dust.

The backlog should be kept within certain time limits. Typically, the length of the backlog should not exceed six months of work, but, as this is mostly very difficult to achieve, even keeping it under 12 months of work is still quite fine.

Line Manager as Product Owner

The Developer-Product Owner relationship usually hurts if the Product Owner is also your Line Manager. In this situation, the developer might be less likely to challenge what the Product Owner says. This is strongly culture and organization dependent. In more hierarchical countries and cultures, having the Line Manager as Product Owner is extremely counterproductive.

Another reason why Line Manager as Product Owner is dangerous is that the Product Owner is part of the Scrum Team, and, as a team member, she should participate the retrospective session, which is one of the principal ways the team learns and improves. But having the line manager present when the team is discussing what mistakes were made and what should be done differently, can sometimes make people very nervous and perhaps lead to people not being so up-front about things that didn't go so well.

Of course, sometimes, it might be necessary to have the Line Manager as Product Owner, perhaps because of special knowledge or customer contacts that she has, or because the organization is very small. In such situations, it would be good if all are aware of the challenges this means for the team and work actively to avoid them.

Product Owner Making All the Decisions

While it's important that the Product Owner is available for the team to make decisions, she should not attempt to make all the decisions. The role of the Product Owner is usually hectic and busy, so she should try to delegate actively as much work and decision making as possible.

Delegating actively means making sure that people know what they can and cannot decide by themselves, that decisions are still communicated, and, most importantly, that people are guided by a common direction and vision and are skilled enough to make good choices.

Full-Schedule Product Owner

It's very easy for the Product Owner to become quite busy. She is usually "in the middle" of the organization. She is, on one hand, being pulled by the development team to the various ceremonies, discussions, and ad-hoc meetings of Scrum. On the other hand, she must often participate in other meetings in product management or other departments that are interested in the development activities. In addition, she sometimes must also coordinate work between other product development teams and their Product Owners, and sometimes also external third parties. Of course, she should also talk to customers or, in some other way, maintain her knowledge of the market, so that she can effectively coordinate backlog item specification and prioritization.

So, quite often, the Product Owner's calendar is full of meetings. The two things that most often suffer as a result are:

1. Customer collaboration
2. Team discussion and backlog item quality

How to avoid this common problem? The Product Owner should learn effective meeting facilitation skills, making the meetings she participates in shorter and more effective. She should also delegate as actively as she can. Finally, she must learn to also say "no" to a meeting request or walk out of a nonproductive meeting.

Product Owner Doing All the Work Herself

It's good that the Product Owner has a practical approach, using the product as much as possible herself. Being involved in testing and usability testing is also good, because it gives experience for the Product Owner on the use of the product. This experience comes in handy when prioritizing errors or new feature requests. However, she should beware of doing too much work herself!

If the Product Owner always takes the role of "principal tester," testing the new features herself, she gains knowledge and can instantly prioritize any findings, but it shows a lack of trust for the rest of the team to do the feature verification. It also coalesces the feature knowledge even more to just the Product Owner. Furthermore, it takes up time, and we already saw in previous mistake that Product Owners' time could be more effectively used elsewhere.

It would be far better to try to find a correct balance in involvement, hands-on work, and detachment and allow the team freedom to deliver. The Product Owner should have enough knowledge on the actual details and usability to be able to instantly prioritize, but she must allow the team to deliver. This increases trust and spreads the knowledge.

The Characteristics of a Good Product Owner

A good Product Owner displays the following characteristics:

- Curiosity
- Respect and Trust
- Helpfulness

Curiosity

The Product Owner should be curious about what's happening in the organization, what's happening with the customers, what other (perhaps dependent) teams are doing, what kind of ideas and concepts are in predevelopment and development. But, also, she's curious about how things are going in her own team – how the new feature that was started in development a couple of days ago is faring. Has the developer met any difficulties implementing the specification?

Being curious allows the Product Owner to communicate and creates situations in which she can fulfill her thirst for knowledge. It also means being a good listener – how can you be curious and ask questions if you're not able to listen when someone answers?

Respect and Trust

A successful Product Owner respects the team members and their expertise and knowledge. Ideally, she also expresses this respect in her comments about the skills and results of individuals in her team. Respect must be transparent in everything that the PO does.

Trust is the other side of the respect & trust coin. These are inseparable. You'll be able to trust people you respect (and show your respect to them actively). They won't fail you.

Respect and trust are inseparable.

Trust also feeds into self-organization. When you show that you trust people, and that you're curious, they'll feel more comfortable showing their situation and plans to confirm that they're on the right path; you empower people to make their own decisions and progress without further "top-down control." It allows the team to maximize the use of the team intellect.

Helpfulness

Although the Scrum Master is the main "impediment remover" for the team, in practice, the Product Owner sometimes needs to assume a similar role. A critical success factor for Product Owners is achieving transparency in the team's eyes, so that the Product Owner is seen to always have an "open-door policy", and that she can answer questions at any time. It's also very important that the Product Owner act in a way that shows she's trying to solve issues that team members might have with any work assignments.

On User Stories

The "Official" User Story Format

Common to most agile methods is the concept of the user story. It's a natural language description of one or more features of the system. The idea is to describe the feature in a language that facilitates discussion between developers and nondevelopers and stakeholders of the project. The discussion enhances everyone's understanding of the specific issue.

There's no "official" user story format; multiple different variations exist. Still, perhaps most popular is the format originally developed by Connextra[7] and popularized by Mike Cohn[8].

7 https://en.wikipedia.org/wiki/User_story
8 https://www.mountaingoatsoftware.com/agile/user-stories

Table 1 The "Cohn" user story format

As a < type of user >,   I want < some goal >   so that < some reason >

The user story isn't a requirement that exhaustively specifies what the system should do or how it should perform. The main purpose of writing user stories is to facilitate discussion. The Product Owner must understand that in addition to the user stories, system requirements, performance requirements, or other types of requirements may also need to be written. User stories shouldn't be misused to be the full specifications of the system.

It's also all right to have backlog items that aren't written in user story format. If these are still called user stories in your tool, it doesn't really matter. As a rule, user stories should be written when there's a clear user of the system involved (such as end user, frequent user, power user, or administrator). But when the work item that needs the development team's attention isn't directly related to a user (e.g., data security requirements or such) there's no need to spend a lot of effort to try to "fit" it into the user story format.

The Importance of Why

Maybe the most important part of the user story is the why; the "so that <some reason>" motivation that drives the user to use the feature. Usually, it's easy to specify features for the system, define who would be using them, and describe how the features should work and what they should do. But the real question for every single story is the "why."

Why does a user want to do something, or does she? The complete sentence of the user story (who, what, and why) should all sound natural. It shouldn't sound like something that the typical user wouldn't likely do.

DEEP Method for Backlog Item Specification

The Product Owner's responsibility is to keep the backlog prioritized, with the highest priority backlog items ready for the team to start working on. As we discussed in the routines chapter, this is done with the help of a regular ceremony, the backlog grooming. Of course, the prioritization and backlog item discussions and specification work happen outside the grooming session as well, but it does offer a regular heartbeat for the backlog maintenance.

A target state for the items on the top of the backlog can be easily remembered with the mnemonic DEEP (see Figure 4).[9]

Let's investigate DEEP a bit deeper!

D.E.E.P

Discussed

Explained

Estimated

Prioritized

Figure 4 The DEEP mnemonic

---

9   The astute reader notices that in his 2010 book: "Agile Product Management with Scrum: Creating Products that Customers Love", Mr. Pichler also defines the acronym DEEP. The version in this book is slightly different but quite similar. Both versions can be used to make sure that backlog items that progress to implementation have been correctly treated by the team and the Product Owner.

Discussed

The top items on the backlog must be discussed with the team. Preferably the whole team, not just some experts. The value in information sharing is core to the agile way of managing work, and there's no better way than to look at the backlog item description and talk about what it means, why it's being done, how it will be implemented, and how it will be tested and verified.

Explained

The backlog item cannot be just a title. A single short sentence might seem understandable, but it almost always won't specify the work item in necessary detail for everyone on the development team. A mandatory rule for any agile teams is that no backlog items are loaded to sprints or started to work on if they only have the title as the description.

If the description is missing, the easiest way to add it is in the backlog grooming (preferred) or sprint planning (last chance!) session. The item should be discussed and the secretary of the session (typically the Product Owner or the Scrum Master) should write down the discussion items to the backlog item, in full view of everyone on the team.

Estimated

Once the item has a description (is explained) and has been discussed, then it should be estimated. This means that whatever method the team uses for effort estimation (ideal hours, story points, etc.) the team estimates how much work it thinks the backlog item is worth. The Planning poker method or a similar "roundtable" of developers works very well with this. You should be slightly wary of having a single developer state how much a story is worth, because it's not always guaranteed that she will have time to actually implement it, and someone else, who might not be as skilled and experienced as she is, might have to implement this story.

Prioritized

Naturally, the top of the backlog must be in fully prioritized order. The firm prioritization should be at least two sprints' worth of items on the backlog. Beyond that, the Product Owner doesn't need to care if the priority order is exactly right.

Backlog Swimming Pool

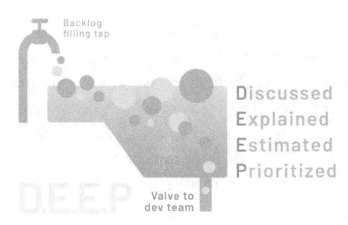

Figure 5
The Backlog Swimming Pool

Traditionally the backlog is seen as a list of items, with the highest priority items on top. If we play a little mind game with the backlog concept, we could turn this idea upside down. Imagine the backlog as a swimming pool, with a shallow end and a slowly DEEPening slope to the DEEP end. In the DEEP end are the items that are ready for implementation and have been DEEP-specified. As you see from the illustration, the items are small and right next to the tap that the development team uses to access the backlog.

The rest of the pool is filled with items that are larger, and in various stages of being specified, split, and "sinking" into the bottom, near the valve that leads to the development team.

The DEEP end of the pool should scare you somewhat, at least until you have learned to dive in. The Product Owner and the people from the development team (preferably all of them) who participate in the grooming sessions should be expert swimmers in the pool. They shouldn't be afraid of the DEEP end. But everyone else? Trying to smuggle something to the top of the backlog? Who knows what lurks in the murky depths of the backlog swimming pool?

The tap that keeps filling the backlog pool usually comes from product management. You'll notice that it has a (yellow) filter. The filter is making sure that only good quality "water" (backlog items) enter the backlog. One of the tasks of the Product Owner is to work with product management on what this filter is like. It typically shouldn't be a single-stage decision point, a go/no go gate to enter the backlog, but rather a process where ideas that might enter the backlog are conceived, tested, and enhanced iteratively until they're confirmed to be good enough to enter the backlog.

Write Stories Together

If it's possible, the Product Owner and the team ideally can write the user stories together. This will instantly share all the information in the story, reduce the need to review and discuss the stories later, and, most importantly, engage multiple brains to think about the issue at the same time.

Obviously, story writing workshops take time to master. Initially, the productivity seems low, but stick with it and the workshops will be smoother and more productive.

If actual story writing sessions don't seem feasible, you can easily also write draft versions of stories yourself, and then have a session (backlog grooming or a specially set up session) to review the new draft stories. The goal for the session then is to review, clarify, and add details to the stories.

User Story Mapping

A perfect tool for these story writing or review sessions is user story mapping. In the user story map, the main functionality areas are outlined on the header row of the map and then the initial row details the most important features. In rows lower down the map, the less important functions are described.

A user story map can be used to brainstorm user stories for a new system and then put them in initial priority order. The stories can, at

Organize Email		Manage Email			Manage Calendar				Manage Contacts		
Search Email	File Emails	Compose Email	Read Email	Delete Email	View Calendar	Create Appt	Update Appt	View Appt	Create Contact	Update Contact	Delete Contact
Search by Keyword *WIP*	Move Emails	Create and send basic email *Done*	Open basic email *Done*	Delete email	View list of appts *Done*	Create basic appt *Done*	Update contents /location	View Appt *Done*	Create basic contact *Done*	Update contact info *WIP*	
	Create sub folders *Done*	Send RTF e-mail	Open RTF e-mail		View Monthly formats *WIP*	Create RTF appt		Accept/ Reject/T entative			**Release 1**
Limit Search to one field		Send HTML e-mail	Open HTML e-mail	Empty Deleted Items	View Daily Format	Create HTML appt	Propose new time		Add address data	Update Address Info	Delete Contact
Limit Search to 1+ fields		Set email priority	Open Attachm ents				Mandato ry/Optio nal				**Release 2**
Search attachm ents		Get address from contacts			View Weekly Formats	Get address from contacts		View Attachm ents	Import Contacts		
Search sub folders		Send Attachm ents			Search Calendar	Add Attachm ents			Export Contacts		**Release 3**

Example story map created by Steve Rogalsky
http://winnipegagilist.blogspot.com

Figure 6 Sample *User story map*[10]

this point, be at a title-level description only. The details can be added when the initial priority has been decided. A sample user story map is shown in Figure 6.

There is a pressure for the Product Owner to "write lots of good user stories" because she feels that that's her responsibility. The Product Owner certainly can take the lead in ensuring that correct stories get done, but it's far better to share the writing load or write stories

10   https://www.barryovereem.com/the-user-story-mapping-game/

together. It's slightly dangerous if the Product Owner writes lots of long, good user stories by herself because then the discussion part, reviewing the stories with the team, takes a very long time and lots of effort. And when something takes a long time and takes lots of effort and everyone is busy, it can be easily forgotten. If stories are written

Write stories together or review and discuss a small number of stories at a time! Avoid having to write a lot of stories for the team to review!

together, or at least if the Product Owner reviews and discusses a small number of stories with the team at any one time, this can be avoided.

Another thing that shouldn't be forgotten is tester involvement. Testers, or at least a representative of testing, should be involved at the beginning. This way, the details that are added to the story description already contain information on how the tester will test the feature. It will also allow the tester to prepare a test environment for when the story arrives at testing.

All of this will speed up the flow of stories through the team's process and reduce waste.

Don't Overspecify

The initial story is only the starting point – a discussion starter. The main benefit for stories is to facilitate the discussion (which then must be documented!). Even after the discussion has happened, and the team feels that they have a good description of the target, stories will continue to improve as the work starts.

A successful Product Owner understands that the specifications aren't final – the understanding of the problem and the best possible solution for it will inevitable get better once the work is ongoing. If a better idea surfaces during the implementation, then everyone in the team, including the Product Owner, should be open to changing the story if it makes more sense.

It's possible that if the user story has too good a description, all the details are already decided in the story-writing stage, then it can potentially reduce the need for creativity during implementation. This could prevent better ideas from appearing. Writing very detailed user stories that are accompanied with full user interface specifications also slows down the story-writing quite a bit. Trying to come up with absolutely everything and writing it down as the user story, takes a lot of time and energy. In a sense, if you give the perfect specifications that are 100% complete to the developer, she'll have very little open issues and questions and will implement it. But you can never be sure if your initial specifications are the best ones.

It's always better to specify enough, but not too much. This allows the developers some freedom, and more easily enables the *small discussions* ceremony (described in Part 3) during the implementation.

Prototypes and MVPs

We've already touched on the importance of testing the ideas before they get to the actual implementation. That doesn't mean that every idea has to go through a similar kind of process. Exactly what is studied needs to be a case-by-case decision done by the Product Manager together with the Product Owner and relevant engineers and stakeholders. When the idea is young, and the business is young, it makes a lot of sense to do more experimenting than when the product is more mature or the business is more mature. When the organization knows its current customers well and is very certain that a feature idea will fly and has enough information to gauge the complete market potential, there's less need to test the idea. In a startup company, on the other hand, the situation is completely opposite; the focus of every action should be in testing the product and business assumptions as quickly as possible, and with as little investment as possible.

Prototypes

There are many ways to gather data about an idea to increase the understanding of the customer problem, but one of the best is to create prototypes to actually show people what the product will do or how the feature will work. The idea with the prototype is that it will take considerably less investment to build and can be done in hours or days. The prototype can also be adjusted extremely fast based on feedback from early tests using it. Prototypes can range from a user interface wireframe all the way to a high definition prototype that looks virtually indistinguishable from a real product. Developing a prototype is a kind of a mini-feature development – you first think what you want to study and who you want to show the prototype to, and then what kind of a prototype can get you the needed information and responses. Does it need to look good? Or does it only need to show the user the features he can access? Does it need to focus on the onboarding – getting users started? Or are there more uncertainties in the actual usability of a key feature? The idea is that the prototypes (and there can be many of them) are focused on exactly the area that needs to be tested.

The prototypes almost always will be throwaway implementation. It rarely makes sense to continue them to be the backbone of the actual product or feature that will be built later. They're developed to test assumptions, confirm the needs and requirements and to increase knowledge. These learnings and the knowledge are then used to define what the real product will be like, the product vision, and the stages how the vision will be built.

Minimum Viable Product (MVP)

The concept of the Minimum Viable Product, MVP, was originally intro-duced in 2001 by Frank Robinson[11], then defined to mean *the sweet spot between how many features to put into the next product release to maximize the return on investment, and the risk or effort on actually including too much and increasing delay*. The term *MVP* has since become ever more popular, and while the business and the world of product development has become more agile, urgent and fast-paced over the following two decades, the term has also evolved.

In the book *The Lean Startup*[12], Eric Ries redefines MVP to mean the *"version of a new product which allows a team to collect the maximum amount of validated learning about customers with the least effort."* This shifts the focus of the MVP from maximizing the business potential to maximiz-ing the learning, and reflects the realities of most startup companies. The "Lean Startup MVP" is also not necessarily an actual product, it can be quite similar to the prototype that was described earlier. It could be a presentation, a video, or a letter as well. The idea is to do something with least possible amount of effort to gain understanding on what to actually build to satisfy the customers and stakeholders.

The most important point that this modern interpretation of MVP makes is that any iteration of the product, be it in prototype form or in the form of an actual release to production use, must aim to increase

---

11 http://www.syncdev.com/minimum-viable-product/

12 https://www.amazon.com/Lean-Startup-Entrepreneurs-Continuous-Innovation/dp/0307887898

the organization's understanding of its customers and their needs. This is something that the Product Owner should also keep in mind. Whenever the Product Manager and the development team think about any release scope, they must also think what they need to learn and how the product release supports that learning. Can they collect data on how customers use the product and it's features such as logs or usage data from online components? Is that data being analyzed? What can they learn from it? If they make a new release, how soon will they learn how customers have received the changes? Do customers like them or not?

You Got an MVP Ready? Wrap It and Ship It!

One risk that the Product Owner must keep in mind if she chooses to use the *Minimum Viable Product* term is that some people may not understand the term in this modern sense. The word *product* and the fact that the term was used widely to describe a production release with maximized business impact might be misunderstood. Some people may also misinterpret the showing of a high definition user interface test "MVP" (which really is a prototype) as a false state of readiness toward actual effort on building said product, and this could result in conflict when the development teams later plans for the actual delivery. For this reason, it might be safer to call any development efforts that are meant for investigations and experiments, as prototypes and prototyping, instead of MVP. The term *MVP* could then be used when the development team is making the actual product based on the information gathered earlier.

Whatever way of using the terms *MVP* and *prototype* you choose to use, just make sure that the organization is clear what the terms mean, and what kind of product or prototype you're building. The important thing is that you think about what you know and what you assume to know, and actually test your riskiest assumptions.

Summary

The mission of the Product Owner is to ensure that the team is working on the most important tasks and that the tasks are clear and well-specified. The goal is to maximize the value that the team can deliver. That means the Product Owner must participate and make sure that the organization does enough testing and iteration of the feature and product ideas before the ideas get to the final implementation queue. Without early testing, the team is guaranteed to waste effort in implementing the wrong things, or implementing things the wrong way.

The Product Owner does this mainly through constant communication with the team, the Product Manager, and other important stakeholders. The Product Owner supports the Product Manager as the main person responsible for early feature discovery. Where the Product Manager makes the high-level prioritization decisions, the Product Owner then takes the ball and makes sure that the delivery works as smoothly as possible, and the final solution is as good as it can be. Good cooperation with the Product Manager is essential. A good Product Owner is

helpful and curious and supports the development team during implementation and takes the role and responsibility of internal customer to
approve the end product.

Now we have seen why Product Owners exist, what they aim to accomplish, and some of the routines, common mistakes and items that they
work on. Next, we will look at how these items of work can be organized into Success Factors that start to show to the reader how to achieve
success in product ownership.

Part 2

The Success Factors

Four-Step Success Factor Model for Product Owners

In Part 1, we looked at why the Product Owner role is so important, and what kinds of routines there are in the day-to-day work. We also looked at some usual challenges or ways to fail and then discussed the user stories which are integral and at the core of what the Product Owner works with.

In Part 2 we'll look at how the Product Owner activities introduced in Part 1 can be arranged into a model of success factors. This success factor model is then used in Part 3 where we'll learn about the 8 Principles for Product Owner success. The success factors define *what* gets done. The 8 Principles in Part 3 tells the reader *how* they can do the activities.

The Major Success Factors

When working in an intelligent way, one starts by creating some sort of a vision or a plan of what to achieve. The next step is to start acting toward that goal. The important bit here is to try to constantly adjust to see if you're achieving good results. Third, you want to get something released. Fourth, you need to evaluate if what and how you work is making sense and decide how you could improve it.

This sounds like the age-old Plan-Do-Check-Act[13] (PDCA) four-step management model, right? That's because it's exactly that. But for Product Owners, the four steps could be more effective if we define them a bit differently.

The first step in the model is the same – *Plan*. Product Owners plan what gets done and in what order based on priority. The agile plan is usually the team backlog. It contains the work, and, implicitly, the schedule.

As the role for a Product Owner isn't to implement anything herself (she has the team to do the implementation), we change the second step in the PDCA model to *"Guide."* Product Owners exist to first prioritize what gets started and then guide the implementation toward a desired goal. They might also use customer testing, demos, tests, or iterations to guide the work to the best possible end state.

The third step is *Release* because defining what and when to release is one of the key responsibilities of the Product Owner and because getting things released, out there, into the hands of the customers is the only way the team and organization can start earning back the value that has been built into the product or service.

---

13   https://en.wikipedia.org/wiki/PDCA

The fourth step in the model is *Learn*. Learning can mean that the Product Owner herself or her team learns to work more effectively, but it can also mean that with the release, they've learned something about the product itself or customers' problems that they can feed into the next iteration, the next planning, implementation, and releasing cycle.

Succeeding in the Product Owner role is the result of how well you can succeed in these four main areas. We'll, therefore, call these four areas the major success factors for Product Owners. The major success factors can be drawn into a wheel as shown in Figure 7. This is the center of the Product Owner's Wheel of Success.

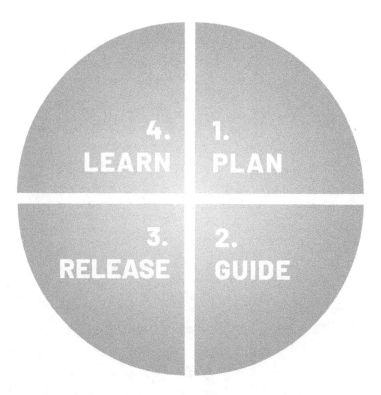

Figure 7 The center of the Product Owner's Wheel of Success with the major success factors

The major success factors are still a bit high-level, so we'll next split each of them to three slightly smaller components. We'll call these success subfactors.

The major success factors are at the center of the Product Owner Wheel of Success. You'll see in the following chapters how the complete Wheel of Success will look like as we expand it with the subfactors and finally the 8 Principles in Part 3.

Success Factor 1: PLAN

The plan in agile is the backlog. This doesn't mean that project plans cannot exist. They can, and are commonly used, especially in cases where the product development isn't only software but also hardware. But for the individual agile team, the only plan that matters is the backlog.

At the core of agile is sustainability. The team should be able to sustain the pace of work indefinitely. It should not spend 14-hour days or work seven days a week for long stints of time to get something urgent done. Ideally, the team shouldn't have urgent work. They should only have work that's prioritized and done with good quality.

That's what the three subfactors for *Plan* aim to convey to the reader. The plan is the backlog, and when working with the backlog items, the Product Owner and the team must always try to think what needs to be done for each backlog item so that it's done with good quality. If the backlog item seems too difficult or too large to specify what good quality means, it must be split further, or clarified and researched further. Teams shouldn't cut corners on quality.

When estimating the effort that the backlog item might take, the team should also further discuss what actually gets done with the item before arriving at a consensus on the probable effort. The value in estimating

Figure 8 Success Factor 1: Plan and its subfactors

is exactly that it encourages discussion of the item. Estimating also prevents the team to start too large backlog items. Starting work on too large items can result in increased error count and difficulties in integration.

The team should not be pressured into taking more than it can get done with good quality. The first two subfactors are, therefore, *Sustainable* and *High Quality*.

Finally, any planning is worthless if it's not coordinated with other teams, dependencies or other activities that are required for a successful product delivery. The Product Owner must understand the big picture of what is required to get the work of the development teams out to the customer and prioritize the backlog in such a way that there are no hiccups. The third subfactor is, therefore, that the plan is *Coordinated*. We can see the three subfactors in Figure 8.

Success Factor 2: GUIDE

Rather than trying to decide everything herself, a good Product Owner tries to delegate as many of the smaller decisions as possible. A good product vision and a valid vision for the currently ongoing release of that product will help in delegating. The vision should be kept fresh, up-to-date and the team and people around the team should know and understand the vision. Then they're able to make small design choices, small decisions on what and how they work every day that take the team and the product in the correct direction without the Product Owner having to intervene in every situation. *Vision Driven* is therefore the first subfactor of *Guide*.

Second, the team and Product Owner must remember that getting early feedback is one of the key ways to shorten development time and get the best possible feature out to the customers. The iterative approach isn't limited to working in sprints. The feature that's being developed must go through constant design iterations that penetrate its whole life cycle. The feature specification should be developed iteratively before it enters the team's backlog, while it's in the backlog, and even while it's under implementation. The small discussions ceremony that we will look at in Part 3 is one of the ways even an ongoing implementation can be guided to the best possible result. The team must use demos and customer reviews, pilots and prereleases effectively to check

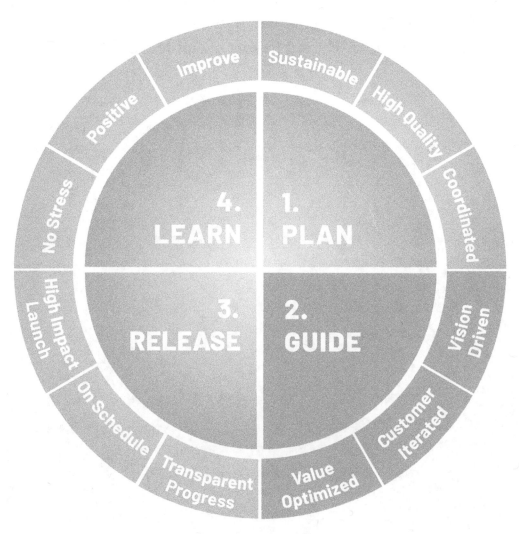

Figure 9 Success Factor 2: Guide and its subfactors

if the feature is specified and implemented in the best possible way. The second subfactor is, therefore, *Customer Iterated*.

Finally, everything that the team does must always maintain the focus on priority. The Product Owner is constantly maintaining the priority order, and as new information comes in, the priority order is regularly updated based on it. The target is moving all the time and the Product Owner needs to keep aiming at the bull's-eye. The third subfactor of Guide is *Value Optimized*. The subfactors of Guide are shown in Figure 9.

Success Factor 3: RELEASE

The progress toward releasing needs to be transparent. A common problem in organizations is that R&D teams are getting undue pressure from other parts of the organization to deliver valuable features. The main reason for getting pressure from outside is that what's being worked on and when it's ready isn't clear to everyone. If everyone outside the R&D teams would know and understand the priority order and the progress toward release, then they wouldn't try to squeeze the team or the Product Owner for more. If the stakeholders felt that they had some new information that affected the priority order, they would take it to the Product Owner and try to affect the plan that way. Keeping the progress toward the release transparent is, therefore, one of the subfactors of *Release*.

What is the schedule for an agile team? The beauty of agile is that there's no "one" schedule. The schedule can be changed freely. The good agile team maintains a constant release capability, developing features and stories iteratively and maintaining near or total production quality at all times. Some organizations release to production multiple times a day. Traditional "on-schedule" doesn't exist in agile. Still, it's the Product Owner's responsibility to think what the optimum time and scope of release is. Some business environments require different process and can result in release once a year or even less frequently. The Product Owner maintains the release plan, and if she is asked to change it, she can state what is possible and when. That's what the subfactor *On Schedule* means.

Getting the results of the team's work out to the customers is the only way the organization really starts to earn back the value of the work. That's why *Release* is the third major success factor. However, unlike in the old saying "build a better mousetrap and the world beats a path to your door," in modern times, having a good product isn't enough. Building the better mousetrap is waste if the organization doesn't support the new release with relevant and powerful coordinated actions. To avoid this waste, the Product Owner needs to make sure that necessary actions for a *High-Impact Launch* are being done elsewhere in the organization, and support them with her personal actions and with the team. The three subfactors for release are shown in Figure 10.

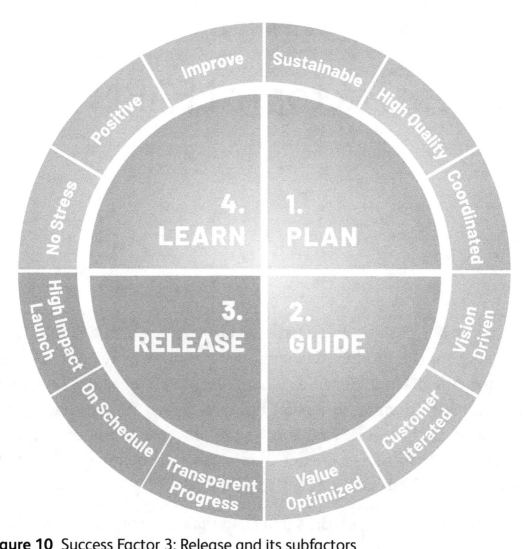

Figure 10 Success Factor 3: Release and its subfactors

Success Factor 4: LEARN

In a successful project, the whole development journey is a learning experience for the Product Owner and the team. The team finds effective ways of working, identifies what needs to change, and sets about changing them. Similarly, a good Product Owner notices patterns in her own work that work well and what she wants to improve. If both the team and the Product Owner are actively improving every day with every sprint and release, it's easy to stay positive.

An improving team that works in a sustainable way feels less pressure from the rest of the organization, and it's easy to stay stress free. This learn-improve-positive-stress-free is a positive spiral that continues to increase the team performance. The three subfactors for this positive learning spiral are therefore *No Stress, Positive, and Improve*. They can be seen in Figure 11.

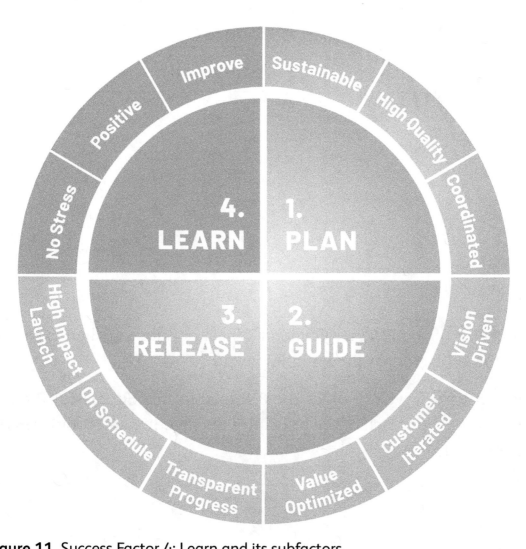

Figure 11 Success Factor 4: Learn and its subfactors

Summary

The center of the Product Owner's Wheel of Success when expanded with the subfactors is shown in Figure 12.

Next, in Part 3, we'll look at the 8 Principles for Successful Product Owners, and how each of the principles fits together and completes the Wheel of Success.

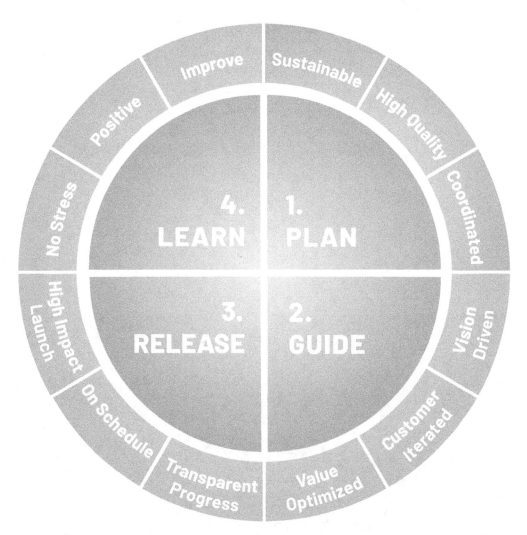

Figure 12 The core of the Product Owner's Wheel of Success with the success subfactors

Part 3

The 8 Principles for Successful Product Owners

Building on the Success Factor Model – The 8 Principles

In Part 2 we introduced the major success factors for Product Owners: Plan, Guide, Release, and Learn. We then looked at the detailed level of each success factor in the form of the subfactors. The major factors and the subfactors give the reader an idea what the Product Owner has to succeed in so that the team gets the maximum value out to the customer. The success factors formed the center of the Wheel of Success.

But exactly how, and in what style, should the Product Owner work to achieve success? That's what the model of the 8 Principles will define. The 8 Principles follow the same chronological order as the success factors, and expand the "big picture." They form the outer rim of the Wheel of Success. Like the rubber tire on the wheel of a bicycle or car, the 8 Principles on the outside of the wheel cushion the ride. Understanding and knowing *how* to work will help the reader achieve a smooth road to success. But if the Product Owner doesn't know enough about the how, the ride isn't so smooth, and any potholes on the way are felt very harshly and can even damage the rim of the wheel itself.

The 8 Principles are:

1. Purposeful Planning
2. Fantastic Feedback
3. Optimal Ownership
4. Team Tactility
5. Mind the Minors
6. Earn and Learn
7. Positivity to Profit
8. Aspire to Improve

The complete Wheel of Success with the 8 Principles added are seen in Figure 13.

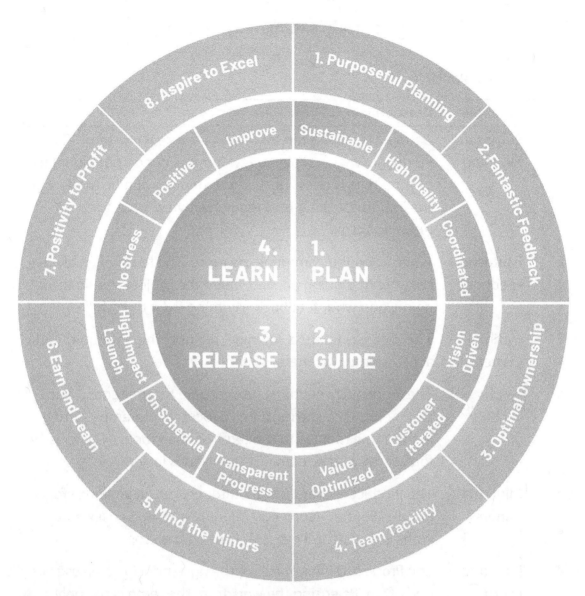

Figure 13 Product Owner's Wheel of Success

The 8 Principles can be quickly summarized in Table 2:

Table 2 The 8 Principles

#	Principle	Description
1	Purposeful Planning	Detailed planning too far into the future is wasteful. The Product Owner can plan a few months ahead but planning beyond that is guessing. Long-term plans can be made, but the important thing is to regularly review what the near future looks like.
2	Fantastic Feedback	When in doubt, communicate more. The team must always know what's going on, and where the project should be going, and what feedback is coming from the market.
3	Optimal Ownership	The role isn't called "owner" for nothing – be bold and act like you *own* the product or service.
4	Team Tactility	The Product Owner must be available for the team. Usually this means that she must be co-located, preferably sitting in the same room with the team. If the Product Owner is farther away, the team effectiveness is lower.
5	Mind the Minors	The Product Owner must maintain constant vigilance for priority. Feature-creep and minor issue fixing easily erodes plans, if a watchful eye isn't kept on the scope.
6	Earn and Learn	The Product Owner must live the agile principle: release early and often. Releasing the work from the team is the only way to start getting the value back to the organization. The team must also constantly develop and improve practices and tools that allow frequent releasing. The team must also remember that any release is an opportunity to learn – how did the released content fare with customers.

#	Principle	Description
7	Positivity to Profit	A happy team is a productive team. As the Product Owner wants the team results and capacity to stay at a high level, she must nurse the team spirit and regularly de-stress the team. Time and money invested in team welfare will return in increased productivity and innovation.
8	Aspire to Excel	Both individual learning of the Product Owner herself, and the team learning on how to improve their ways of working, communication, tools, and methods is essential in ensuring that the team succeeds and improves.

In the following chapters, we'll look at how the 8 Principles help the Product Owner achieve success with the project or product.

Principle #1:
Purposeful Planning

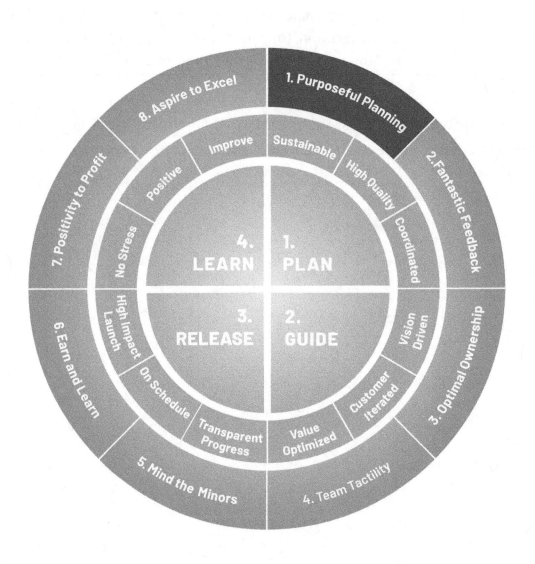

WHAT IT MEANS:

In the agile way of working, the traditional project plan with detailed schedules has very little value. *Purposeful Planning* means that the Product Owner continuously maintains a prioritized list of well-specified backlog items and a clear idea of what gets released when. Detailed planning is done to the near future work only. Activities that happen many months or even years in the future aren't forgotten but receive much less attention. All activity is driven by a common and shared vision.

BEWARE:

The Product Owner should be aware of the following risks:

- Planning too far into the future in too great a detail.
- Allowing unspecified, undiscussed items to progress into implementation.
- Allowing too large items to progress into implementation.
- Failing to communicate transparently to all stakeholders what the current plan is.

The Death of the Gantt Chart

Before things turned agile, the best friend of the Project Manager was the project plan with its schedule in Gantt chart format. When things were planned using the waterfall model, a lot of effort was spent early in the project to create a detailed plan, a sequence of events that would lead to a successful project. The planning of the project and the detailed Gantt chart felt like a holy ceremony – somehow putting the different stages of the project on paper would change it from wishful thinking to reality.

Today, you very rarely see a Gantt chart or a massive project plan in projects that have mostly software development activities. Project plans and Gantt charts still exist, especially in hybrid projects which have a lot of non-software development effort.

For example, if the project contains mechanics, production facilities, training, or documentation activities, it's much easier to define what should be done and how long it takes. In these applications, the project plan and the detailed schedule are still valuable, mainly because the much more predictable nature of the activities makes planning much easier and much less likely to be continuously under drastic changes. In these cases, the plans and planning have value and it makes sense to continue doing them. On software creation side, where level of uncertainty is much higher, the world has moved on.

The Purposeful Plan

How do successful Product Owners then plan and estimate what gets done when? It all starts from understanding what the team's or organization's speed of implementing production quality code is – the velocity. Simply put, the velocity means the average amount of work that the team actually finishes in any given time. The important word is *finishes*. The team must have a solid definition of *done* to make sure that when items are marked as closed or done, they're as close as possible to production quality. The team and the Scrum Master are usually experts in velocity measurement.

Purposeful plan is an educated guess based on facts – velocity and estimated, prioritized backlog.

Velocity

Velocity is always calculated from the estimated effort, not the realized effort. This is because you're using the velocity value to compare to other estimated efforts – the backlog. Therefore, they must be done in the same way. If you always estimate in the same way, it doesn't matter if the actual effort is higher. If both the velocity and the effort estimates on the backlog are done in the same way, any estimates are as reliable as they can be. If you used actual effort for velocity calculation, and estimated effort for backlog items, you'll always get incorrect results. That's why it's generally recommended not to even track actual effort at all, unless it's done for some other purpose, such as resource bottleneck identification or reporting of work hours.

The Product Owner should have quite an intimate understanding of the team's velocity. No matter if the team uses Scrum (velocity is the average amount of completed backlog items per sprint) or Kanban (the average can be calculated per week or per month), the Product Owner must understand what the team is capable of right now. Scenarios can be created on how team growth affects the velocity, but be very careful with these; proven, historical, data-based velocity is usually the best metric to follow.

For any given sprint, the velocity value can jump from quite low values (even zero!) to high, depending on whether the team actually finished any tasks. Meaningful velocity values are always calculated as a rolling average over many sprints or weeks. Usually, a rolling average over 4 sprints or 8 weeks gives a very accurate idea on the current speed of implementation.

Velocity can change over time as the teams learn to work better, or if the team composition is changing. This should be considered when planning. However, when teams learn to work more effectively, they also unconsciously start to estimate effort of tasks differently. A task that previously had 5 story points now only has 2. This is one further reason to avoid estimating the backlog too far into the future. Estimates that are very old are at risk of being inaccurate.

The Road to the Release

The road to the release is like a journey. The scope of the release is the remaining travel distance. The velocity is how fast you're going at the moment. With the remaining distance and the velocity known, it's easy to calculate how long it will take to get there. In Figure 14 below, you can see the release scope as a blue bar on the left (representing the backlog of the release, in prioritized order) and then the velocity of the

Figure 14 Visualization of the velocity eating the release scope – and the code complete and maturation period before release capability

team as small white boxes. At code complete at the end of the implementation, there's always some period when the product is verified and the release is prepared. This is called the maturation period.

If you think of it like this, then you can usually forecast the schedule of the release quite accurately. The potential factors that can vary the final outcome are:

1. If your velocity is subject for large changes (development team personnel changes).
2. If your maturation period is unknown or likely to be significantly different compared to previous releases.
3. If your backlog items have not been completely and exhaustively specified, then the initial estimate that you have on them might be off.
4. If there is high risk of backlog priority changes or new backlog entries yet unknown that would go high up on the backlog priority order.

Out of the above, the team velocity is usually quite stable. Teams can improve their performance, and they should, but this rarely increases their velocity significantly. As we described earlier, this is due to the feedback loop in the estimation process; as a team improves, the team members start to assign lower estimated effort for tasks that they now find easier. So, this leads to the velocity being near the same, even though the team actually achieves more. This fact is also why the backlog estimations that have been done a long time ago (a year ago, or longer) are usually almost worthless. It's much better to split larger stories into smaller stories closer to the time of implementation, maximum 2 to 4 months before implementation. This way, the estimates for the final stories are much closer to the velocity.

The maturation period means the time between the last new implementation finished and the release. In a perfect agile organization, where all the tests are automated, this time is quite short. However, test automation coverage very rarely reaches 100%, and, typically,

Effort estimates have a best before date – estimating items that won't get done in next 3–4 months is wasteful.

at least some manual testing is needed. Also, other activities that the development team or somebody else needs to do can delay the release.

The length of the maturation period depends on answers to several questions:

- Is the product a brand-new product or an evolution of a mature product?

- Is the team a new team or a mature, well-formed team?
- Is the product a consumer product or a customizable product for enterprise users, or a project delivery for a single customer?

What is the industry? Some industries (such as pharmaceutical, medical, or aerospace) have much higher quality requirements than others and this affects the amount of testing, requirement traceability, documentation, and allowed amount of errors in the releasable product.

The third item, the error in the effort estimate in the large, unsplit backlog items, can cause more variance in the release estimate. A good way to reduce the likelihood of this is to regularly discuss and review the large items on the backlog that still belong to the release scope, and when the time is right, actively split them to smaller stories with detailed descriptions and effort estimations.

Another way is to do research studies called Spikes.[14] Spikes are small investigations into a problem, issue, or technology that aim to find out how much effort the necessary implementation would take. Spikes can add detail, help in splitting the items to smaller stories, and reduce technology risk. With active backlog grooming and Spikes, the impact of the third point on the release estimate can be kept in check.

The final, potentially highest impacting risk for the release estimate uncertainty is any new, late-arriving must-have requirements or changes. These always add work to the release. The only way to reduce the impact of these or avoid them altogether is to actively test the

---

14   https://en.wikipedia.org/wiki/Spike_(software_development)

product assumptions as early as possible. Such testing of the ideas and specifications should happen in the product management process before the items ever reach the actual product backlog. But even when they're in the backlog, or under development, a successful Product Owner uses many methods for getting feedback on her plans. We'll discuss more about the feedback aspect in the next chapter.

Of course, the larger the release scope is, and the longer the duration of the implementation, the larger the uncertainty in any schedule estimate will be. As we have discussed earlier, it's best to keep the detailed backlog analysis and effort estimates focused to the top 2–3 months of the backlog. If your release scope is beyond this, 6–12 months or even longer, you'll have much higher schedule uncertainty! There's no way to avoid this. If you try to analyze the backlog completely with details in each of the stories and estimated effort for all the tasks, you'll spend a lot of time, but the actual details and effort estimates will actually "get old" and expire like old milk in the fridge. By the time the team gets around to starting work on them, they'll be both unfamiliar, forgotten, and probably needing redefinition. It's much better to focus your efforts in the near future, and try to convince and coach the organization for smaller more frequent releases. If smaller public releases aren't possible, then you should try to plan for internal release increments that lead to the final product being available later, and just accept the schedule or scope uncertainty that results from this approach.

When Will It Be Ready?

It's the Product Owner's responsibility to maintain the targeted release scope and schedule. But quite often, she gets the statement: "That's much too late; we need to have the release out by November. What can we have by then?" In this situation, the Product Owner must estimate what could be done by the requested deadline.

In Figure 15, you can see what the Product Owner could answer to such a question. She would take the top of the backlog and calculate back from the new requested release date minus the expected maturation period. Then she could let the person know the answer – in the case of the example, about half of the scope of the original release could be delivered.

Does the maturation period change when we cut the scope this way? This can be discussed with the team, but any change is likely to be quite minor.

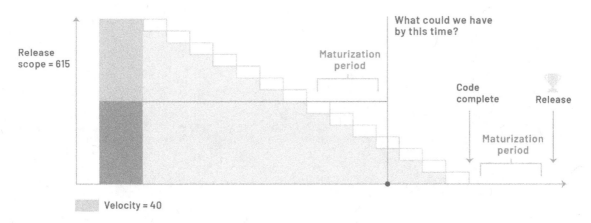

Figure 15 Visualization of the question of an earlier release date

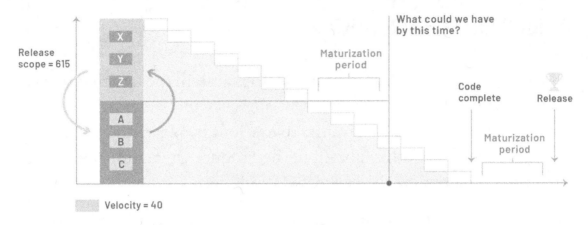

Figure 16 Exchanging A, B and C to the requested X, Y, and Z

The shorter time-to-deliver results in significant reduction of the release scope. The next question usually is something like: "That's not good enough; can we have X, Y and Z included?" Again, the Product Owner can estimate that scenario as well, but it's not possible to add something to the scope without removing something else, so adding X, Y and Z could work as in Figure 16: A, B and C are postponed.

If it's not possible to postpone anything, then it looks like in Figure 17.

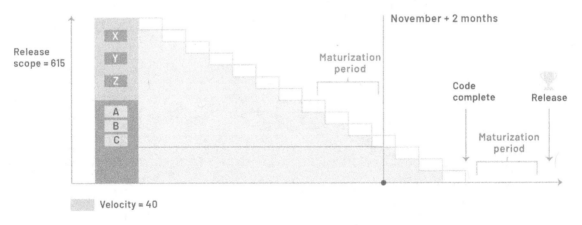

Figure 17 Both X, Y and Z and A, B and C are mandatory

The final question that the Product Owner often gets is, can the team somehow increase the velocity? Maybe by hiring consultants or new personnel? Maybe by doing things more "effectively?" Introducing new persons to a software project generally slows things down, and then speed increases later (if the team doesn't grow to be too large). In other words, new resources don't often help short-term. If the target is further away than a year, then new resources typically do increase velocity significantly, after a time. But this is typically beyond the short-term release planning and more in the realm of roadmapping.

Of course, it's possible to work more effectively and increase the team's velocity, but usually these changes aren't big, nor are they fast. Good use of retrospectives for team-internal learning and coaching of the team can be approaches to speed things up. We'll talk more about these when we look at principle 8.

Probably only one scenario can increase velocity significantly, and that's if persons can be found elsewhere from the organization who have in recent months been working with the product. They still have the skills and familiarity to assist instantly. They probably are also instantly familiar with the company culture, ways of working, process and even the people. But as a general guideline, velocity changes cannot be used for changing the release schedule – compared to changing the scope, they have only minor impact.

Keeping Things Simple

What can be used and should be used to change the schedule, is strict pruning of the release scope, the backlog items that are planned to be in the release. The items can and should be simplified when there is high schedule

Adding developers to a late software project makes it later.[15]

pressure. It's very common to have significant room for simplification in the backlog items – remove fancy user interfaces, remove rarely used options for end users, and so on. This makes implementation easier, but it significantly simplifies testing and leads to a much lower amount of errors in the product, which, in turn, shortens the maturation period.

Making things simpler is a very powerful way to ensure that a project doesn't get delayed. Where adding developers usually slows things down, removing features or making features work in a simpler way usually leads to significantly faster implementation and testing. As with everything else, also the simplification should be done transparently, with full product management knowledge, so that there are no surprises late in the project.

Start It or Split It?

Items at the top of the backlog should be estimated, and the team should have a firm rule on the maximum value of effort before they'll

15 Fred Brooks – The Mythical Man Month, 1975

Starting too large backlog items is a sure way for lower quality, more errors, and a delayed project. Teams that use effort limits achieve better results.

start without splitting it into two or more separate items. This is because without any firm limit, the team can try to fit too large a story into a sprint, and they won't be able to finish it in the sprint.

Another reason for limiting story size under a specific maximum is that with shorter stories, the people who have a tester role in the team have faster access to new sprint deliverables ready for testing once a sprint starts. With too large stories, the testing is all bunched up against the final days of the sprint, and this always leads to "mini waterfall" integration and testing difficulties, creating delays at the end of the sprint in making the sprint release. With smaller stories, it's also much easier to do accurate effort estimates and test plans.

One rule of thumb could be that if the sprint length is two weeks (10 working days) then no story should be planned to take over 5 days, and the team should target stories that are 2–3 days long. The team should set an initial effort limit and then experiment with what limit seems to work best. Shorter limits force the team to split stories more often. This results in more discussion and smaller work items. Story-splitting is a skill of its own and should be practiced with the Scrum Master and the Scrum team until it becomes a routine.

Supersized Stories

If the top of the backlog should be "ready-to-digest" stories that are small enough and DEEP, then the rest of the backlog can contain items of varying size and detail. The backlog grooming ceremony is the place where team focuses on the rest of the backlog and adds detail, discusses, estimates, and checks the priorities.

Sometimes the team knows that it has to work on some larger feature later, but hasn't yet found the time to specify it fully or split it into individual stories. In this situation, the team can enter an EPIC or a large story to the backlog. It would be good for the Product Owner and the team to agree on some way of marking the large story on the backlog as a "placeholder" story – it needs much more clarification and splitting work before it can be accepted for implementation. The Product Owner could use the state "New" or "Draft" of the story in whatever tool is used to communicate this. Naturally, draft level stories should not exist at the top of the backlog. If they do, they must, as soon as possible, be refined into implementable stories in backlog grooming sessions or, at the latest, in the sprint planning session.

However, there are benefits in discussing and giving even large, unclear stories some effort estimates. For example, if a typical story would be from 1 to 13 story points, then a large story could be 50-100 story points in size. This could exist in the backlog and be marked into the release. Having the story in the release would allow the Product Owner to have a release burndown or burnup chart that has at least some estimation on the release schedule. It would of course be much better that the release includes fewer large stories, and the Product Owner does well to make it quite clear to everyone who is interested in the schedule that it's based on a certain level of supersized stories. In fact, it's an interesting metric to follow; if the team is able to analyze and split the supersized stories in coming months, then the schedule estimate and the associated "level of supersized stories in the estimate" becomes more and more accurate and trustworthy. This is a good way to educate the organization on the method of gaining the schedule estimate based on effort and velocity.

Don't Get Stuck in the Too-Long-Backlog-Swamp

The backlog should not grow to be too long and large. Managing a backlog that has many hundreds or even thousands of items in it becomes slow and painful. Since the Product Owner works with the backlog almost daily, she doesn't want the work to be slow and painful! A long backlog will also mean that urgent work cuts ahead of planned work quite often. The low priority items near the bottom of the list never get done, and they become outdated. Managing such a backlog starts to feel tedious, and this leads to even more items gathering dust. You can see the negative spiral such a backlog would have on the planning?

It would be better to clean out the low priority tasks or not allow them to enter the backlog at all. They could exist in a separate wish list that's regularly reviewed with product management and senior developers, but the frequency of the wish list review can be once a month or even once a quarter.

Sometimes, the bottom of the backlog contains a large number of minor small requests for usability improvements that are difficult assign a business value, but perhaps combining many such requests into a single "EPIC" will make a nice feature. Such small improvements could be best implemented when they can find a suitable "big brother" in some other new feature that touches the same feature or functionality area. Then they're also easier to communicate to customers because customers are already listening in and focused to the same feature.

To be able to do velocity-based release estimation and burndown charts, it's still good to try to have all work in the current release in the backlog. If the release is 1–2 years from now, and there's a risk that the backlog grows too long, the Product Owner could try several different strategies:

• Split the work to subreleases, and only specify the closest subreleases in the backlog.
• Use large stories and EPICs for grouping work into larger entities, as this will reduce the backlog item count.
• Fight in the organization to release more frequently; 1-2 years is a lot of time. Is your organization certain that the release couldn't be made earlier with less content?

It would be good to keep the backlog length at 3-6 months. If the backlog is much longer than that, items at the bottom are so far into the future that there's very high risk that more important work is discovered before they ever progress into implementation. Any prior analysis on items this far in the future will be always out of date by the time they eventually get under implementation, requiring the team to do analysis again with the latest information. This leads to wasted effort and undermines people's motivation to participate in the planning and estimation process.

Inherited a long backlog

Okay, let's imagine a situation in which you've just started as Product Owner and the backlog from the previous owner is very long. The best thing to do is to clean it out. Throw out old, low-priority items (they will surface again for sure if they were critical to someone!), combine some stories to larger stories to reduce the backlog item count, and move some items to a wish list state. These methods allow you to reduce the number of items on your backlog to a manageable number, and you can then actually start working with the team to make sure that the items themselves are of good quality and the top of the backlog is DEEP specified.

Inherited an Empty Backlog

This happens more rarely, but it might be that with some projects that are just starting up, the backlog doesn't contain enough work items. The thing to do then is to have a workshop with the development team, based on the product vision, to identify what needs to be built or, if that can't be specified yet, what needs to be studied and investigated so that the necessary knowledge to specify what needs to be built can be attained.

"Clear" Means Empty Only on the Firing Range

The backlog items must be well-specified. A very common problem is that everyone assumes that an item is clear and without possibility for misunderstanding, so it's left with only a title or a single sentence description. This is a big mistake. It's guaranteed that, unless an item is written down in the form of title, description, and details, it will have multiple different interpretations. This will lead to constant discussions within the team about what the story actually contained. This discussion must take place in the grooming or planning sessions, and be documented into the story description. Allowing empty stories to progress to implementation just invites conflicts and extreme difficulties in completing tasks within the planned time. Nobody will know when the items are completed because the acceptance criteria haven't been documented!

As we saw with the DEEP method, the items just have to be discussed and the discussion documented. Conversation is essential! The best way to have the conversation is to write the stories together in a workshop-like setting. Although this might seem as inefficient use of the team's or expert's time, it will save time in the end.

Finally, the backlog item specs should be transparent to all of the team members and stakeholders. Stakeholders, other team members, and other teams with dependencies must know what will be implemented. Curiosity and more eyeballs on the backlog items will increase the accuracy, quality, and robustness of the backlog items and, eventually, the final product.

Cultivate a Systematic Approach to Troubleshooting

Most of the work performed by the development team is grouped as user stories or bugs. Some teams prefer also to list isolated tasks in backlog. Whatever the name of the backlog item, the important thing is that it has a clear description. A good description is an essential starting point to creating good solutions. We'll look at the bugs first and, after that, the new feature development, tasks, and stories.

An example of an ideal error report is shown in Table 3.

All of the above information is usually necessary for a fast bug investigation and resolution. It's quite common that, unless there is good bug-reporting discipline, the report doesn't contain all essential information. People leave information out because they're in a hurry or they assume that the developers know or can guess the missing information.

The Product Owner should make sure that only good quality bug reports enter the development team process. This responsibility can, of course, be delegated to a QA Manager, or the team can agree on rules on what kind of errors are taken into the fixing process.

For example, if the test steps are unclear or missing, the developer who gets assigned the error will only start to test how the error situation could be reproduced, but, without the steps, she will soon likely give up and either work on something else or assign the error back to the originator for more information. In the worst case, the situation becomes a ping-pong game of "I can reproduce it every time" and "it works on my computer." The Product Owner should make sure that the persons in the team who are doing the testing, really understand and want to fill

Table 3 The ideal error report

Information	Description
Title	A short and clear title.
Severity	Severity (fatal/showstopper, critical, major, minor).
Tested on	Information on what version it was tested on (Software under Test, SUT).
Environment	Information on the environment where it was tested.
Preconditions	Preconditions for the reproduction steps.
Steps to reproduce	Reproduction steps with which the bug can be reproduced.
Expected result	What was the expected result based on specification or tester intuition.
Actual result	What was the actual result.
More information	More information on the error:
When	When it was first noticed.
Where	Where it was first noticed (environment, version).
Recovery information	How the end user can recover from the error situation.
Reproducibility	How often the error is reproduced (every time, easily, hard to reproduce, cannot reproduce).
When not	When is the error not encountered (different execution steps, different environment, time of day, etc.).
Originator	Originator (who first reported the error, if it's not the person creating the error ticket, with contact information)

in all the information in the table above. This will speed up the developer reproducing the error and fixing it.

It would be possible to adjust the error-reporting tool to have all the above fields as mandatory fields, but this could backfire; it makes the error reporting slightly more laborious. Thus, people who don't often report errors dislike using the tool so much that they avoid reporting errors because it's too much work. It's generally better to try to coach the organization's most frequent error originators to fill in all the above information into the existing error description fields.

Another thing to avoid is jumping too early into assumptions or conclusions on what could be causing the error. In a systematic troubleshooting approach, after the problem has been defined as described above, the developer tries then to find all alternative root causes that could have resulted in the error situation. Then the alternatives are tested in the order of likelihood. In most cases, when the alternatives are listed, the one that's most likely to cause the problem is usually the root cause.

Ping-pong errors create waste.

Sometimes, developers have a "favorite" reason for something that they cannot easily explain: "that's a buffering issue," "that's because the device wasn't rebooted." It's easy for the human mind to seek an easy way out of a difficult situation, and these "favorite" root causes are a sure sign that a more systematic way to investigating the problem is needed.

Another sign that a more systematic approach is needed is if you have a lot of so-called "Zombie bugs." A Zombie bug is one that's supposedly fixed, and, initially, it seems to disappear, but then it comes back again. What has usually happened in these cases is that the developer didn't understand the root cause, made a "guess," and then attempted a fix. If this happens a lot, a systematic study should be started.

If you have a lot of Zombie bugs it means you should try to improve the systematic way of fixing errors.

The work on the bugs starts from the initial error report. As a Product Owner, you should make sure that you see every error and make sure that any error that the development team works on has all or most of the information that was listed in Table 3.

Although it's generally better to not make decisions that are based on opinions but base any action on facts, sometimes, the role of Product Owner requires you to take decisive action. This is especially important if there seems to be competing and differing stances within the team on how to fix something. If there is a difference of opinion on what option should be chosen, the Product Owner can jump in and make a decision. In such a situation, it's important to explain as clearly as possible the reasoning behind the decision, so that people who were supporting the other option don't feel that their voice wasn't heard. Generally, it would be better for the Product Owner to clearly define the criteria for choosing the way a bug is fixed and then let the team select the approach. But if this doesn't seem to work, then the decision is needed. In the team retrospective, the team can then discuss why they couldn't agree on an approach to fix without the Product Owners involvement.

Share the Specification With Stakeholders

One of the agile values is transparency, and, in the spirit of transparency, the Product Owner should make sure that the project stakeholders know what the team intends to do. This not only means the current and next Scrum sprint, but also the entire backlog. The Product Owner should find out an effective method of sharing the progress and outcomes of the story writing.

This is closely related to whatever process the product management uses for idea development. Good cooperation with product management is required. When describing the backlog items to stakeholders, some creativity is usually required because the items don't yet exist in the form of an implementation. Anything that's visual will capture people's attention far better than words. User interface prototypes, paper models, wire-frames, or similar ideas are much better than sending a written description for stakeholders to review. If at all possible, showing any such prototypes one-on-one to stakeholders is infinitely better than a meeting, demo session, or email. In a one-on-one session, you can be sure that the stakeholder has actually focused on, looked at, or tried the prototype and has understood the issue.

If a one-on-one session isn't possible, another way to do the sharing is with the regular newsletter that we described earlier in the routines section. However, with an email, you can't be sure who has read it and who has not. The Product Owner should know who specifically should be aware of each backlog item's progress throughout the process. To assist in this, it would be a nice addition to the user story or backlog item to state who originally requested it or who might be impacted by it. This way, months (hopefully not years!) later, the Product Owner could easily recall who she needs to check with whether the updated description is still correct.

Equally important, as a clear specification, is the priority order. The natural tendency of any person who has requested anything from the R&D team is to assume that her request is actually quite high on the list of priorities. As the Product Owner must make the complete prioritization of all such requests, it's more than likely that everyone's request isn't top priority. Unless the Product Owner transparently communicates what is the position of the request on the backlog, and when it perhaps could enter implementation and release (if ever), people will assume that their requests are higher on the list than they actually are. This could result in conflict when the team makes releases in the future. The Product Owner is responsible for communicating in a way that people understand where their request is on the backlog.

The Wheel of Success and Principle #1

If the plan looks too far ahead, the likelihood of it being realized is low. That's why, in the purposeful plan, we don't look too far into the future. Events in the purposeful plan are likely to happen. The plan is trustworthy, and everyone knows what the plan is, so it's very useful in coordinating activities.

However, as the plan doesn't look too far into the future, it needs to be constantly maintained. The regular communication needed between team members and different stakeholders keep everyone on the same page and allow for constant opportunities to adjust the direction of the project.

Summary – the Five Key Points

1. Understand the team velocity and be ready and willing to instantly use it to estimate potential release scopes and schedules.
2. Maintain the top of the backlog in good order (DEEP: Discussed, Explained, Estimated, Prioritized).
3. Avoid building too long a backlog, and if you've inherited or built one that's too long, trim it down.
4. Work with product management to have a process that will continuously fill the backlog with high quality new backlog items. These ideas and features should be already well tested, but they don't need to be DEEP specified yet.
5. Keep everybody, the team, the stakeholders, even the customers, regularly informed about the current release schedule and content.

Principle #2:
Fantastic Feedback

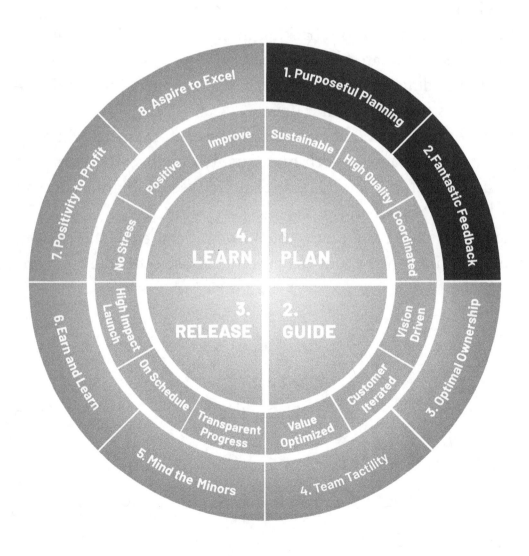

WHAT IT MEANS:

Giving and getting *Fantastic Feedback* is one of the core competences of a successful Product Owner. Product Owners must make sure that the stakeholders and customers are aware of what's going on and are given enough opportunities to give feedback on plans, ongoing implementation and released solutions.

As well as the feedback on team deliverables, the Product Owner must also listen to what the team is telling her. She should have an open ear regarding improvement proposals coming from retrospectives and other meetings. She should also not be biased to her own ideas and dismiss ideas from others in regards to items on the backlog. She should maintain curiosity and allow the team to raise solution health related issues to the backlog.

Every communication opportunity should be viewed as an opportunity for getting feedback on the most important aspects of the project and product; the backlog items, the priorities, and one's own and the team's capabilities and performance.

BEWARE:

The Product Owner should be aware of following risks:

- Trusting that by talking to some customers directly, you get a complete market view.

- Focusing too much on backlog items that add functionality and features and forgetting to listen to developer's wishes to refactor the solution.
- Not giving enough encouragement and positive feedback for the team.

Constant Communication with the Team

There are many things that the Product Owner must remember to communicate to the team and to the stakeholders: the vision, decisions, specification of the backlog items, project and release plans to name but a few. It's good if the Product Owner plans ahead on how to do this communication. However, plans can only get you so far. Keeping the communication regular is far more important than doing it based on a good plan. Nowhere is this more important than in communicating with the implementing teams. This should happen regularly, every day.

Remembering to constantly communicate, keeping the team informed about where the project currently is, where it's heading, and where it SHOULD be heading is perhaps the most important enabler for allowing the individual team members to make small decisions and choices that will help the team toward the common goal.

Constant communication and a shared vision enable a self-organizing team and makes delegating decision making easier.

Common daily sessions also allow you, as the Product Owner, to take the stage and continue to sell your vision of the product to the team. Remember, communication isn't a one-way street. As important as it is to tell the team where the product is, the Product Owner must remain open to ideas, feedback, questions, and observations from the team.

Your objectives for team communication should be:

- Everyone in the team knows all the time the project and product vision and the current release targets.
- Everyone in the team is aware of the latest customer feedback on the product and is hungry for more feedback and continuous improvement.
- Everyone in the team has a reasonable grasp of the big picture – what the other people and other teams are working on, what's going to happen next, and what the current challenges are.
- You manage to activate people's creativity and engage them for ideas and improvement potential.
- You maintain an open-door policy for questions, comments, and improvement ideas. You listen actively to anyone who approaches you with ideas, concerns, and comments.

Active Listening

Successful Product Owners can utilize the full brainpower and observational power of their teams. This is only possible if you show with all your actions that you want your team to think, comment, observe, and bring to your attention any piece of information that might affect the product or project. In practice, this means that when somebody approaches you with a suggestion, comment, a worrying piece of information, or an improvement idea, you should drop whatever you're doing, turn to face her or ask her to sit down, and actively listen. You must always act like you value the opinions and suggestions from others.

If, however, you act like you don't want to listen to her right now, that you're busy, the person will feel that she or her input isn't important. This will mean that, in the future, this person will:

- Take less initiative.
- Think less about the ways to ensure the product success.
- Have a higher threshold for coming to you with a suggestion or an idea.

This is difficult, especially given the usually busy schedule of the Product Owner. Still, the value in such ideas and feedback from the project members is too great to ignore.

When someone approaches you, you must listen. If your day seems to be filled with meetings, one solution to this is to clear out a time slot after the team daily standup. 30 minutes could be enough. This allows team members to have a daily opportunity to come to you for comments, ideas, or questions,

Encourage your team to make suggestions – and make sure they realize even a rejected suggestion is a good achievement!

and it allows you to give the team your complete attention. This must be repeated for all the teams that are working for your product.

If you don't have enough time to listen, if you fill your schedule with meeting after meeting, one of the things you'll miss, is time with your team. With a busy schedule, you're instantly not as approachable as you should be. People are less likely to wander to your desk with a proposal if you're constantly running to the next meeting. And, if someone does think that she has something to tell you, you yourself will feel "too busy" to give the person your full attention. Think about it – if someone comes to you with a suggestion, but you continue working on your computer without giving her your full attention, and with a few seconds to think about it, you dismiss her idea as unrealistic or low priority. That person will feel like her idea wasn't very good. She will be very unlikely to come up with more proposals in the future.

To successfully engage the team to think, you have to show them that you'll always stop to listen when they have something to say. Consider every proposal equally. When you think that the proposal was perhaps not important enough to be put on the backlog, you must explain, based on the product and release vision, why this is so, and still you must remember to thank the person for the idea. You can also explain that a rejected idea isn't a failure – lots of ideas get rejected. Encourage your team to make suggestions and to think about improvements – and make sure they understand even a rejected idea is a victory!

Power of Encouragement

It's natural for people to hesitate when they have to do something that they're not completely familiar with, or which feels a bit scary. In new product development, your team members will need to occasionally investigate new technologies, look at source code that they're unfamiliar with, or complete tasks that previously were done by somebody else, perhaps with more experience.

In the agile spirit, the Product Owner (or anyone else for that matter) cannot and should not assign tasks or force someone to start to work on something. The team should commit to the tasks together and individuals should volunteer to take tasks. However, the Product Owner can be an encouraging voice that helps the team or person to start the task at hand. Rather than force the team to take something, the Product Owner should communicate the urgency of the task and why it's needed, and then offer her full support and encouragement for the team or person to start it. But this cannot be done in a way where the Product Owner "doesn't take no for an answer" – she must be sensitive enough to listen if there really is something that's blocking the team from doing the task.

The best way to encourage others is to inspire them with your own actions. Whenever possible, pull your own weight and show an example.

People Crave Acknowledgement

It's a built-in desire in everyone – we crave feedback. Whenever we do something, we like to show it to others and then we really desire to get feedback on our results. Think about it; this is what Facebook and all the other social media success stories are built on; people post what they've done, and then they await comments and likes from their friends. This is how humans work. People like positive feedback, and they gravitate toward doing things that they receive positive feedback from. Why is it then that in modern workplace, we have far too little feedback and acknowledgement?

It's possible that the move to a more self-organized way of working, as promoted in the agile principles, has actually reduced the amount of feedback in the workplace. Traditionally, the manager was assigning tasks to employees, and then monitoring and following up on the progress. This gave a clear opportunity to congratulate people for a job well done. When, in agile, we now remove the manager, and people "volunteer" to take tasks, who is there to give them feedback when they do something?

The obvious answer is that the team or the other team members should do it. But especially in newly formed teams, teams that are new to agile, teams that have an inexperienced Scrum Master, or teams that don't understand the value of feedback and positive thinking, it's very possible that the level of feedback that people get is far too low. This has a serious impact on how well the team can achieve its maximum potential capacity; therefore, the level of feedback is a concern also for the Product Owner.

What Product Owner should do is, together with the Scrum Master, coach the team on the value of giving feedback, and make sure that the team builds customs and habits of giving appreciative feedback early and often. A nice and concise book on the value of well-timed feedback is the classic *The New One Minute Manager*[16] by Spencer Johnson.

Feedback from Stakeholders and Customers

As challenging as communicating and getting and giving feedback to the team is, getting feedback from customers and other stakeholders is even more difficult. It just happens to be one of the most critical factors of the product and project success.

All product development is built on assumptions. All user stories are assumptions. You assume this is what the users want. Even the smallest detail on a user story can be seen as a guess. When writing the story, you're guessing that this thing is exactly what the end users want. You're also guessing on the priority order. One can never have complete certainty on what the correct priority order is. You're just guessing, based on what market information you have and what customer contacts you have.

The more customers you contact and the more frequently you can communicate with them, the more opportunities you have on gathering feedback on individual story details, the priority order of features,

16 https://www.amazon.com/New-One-Minute-Manager/dp/B00WIZZZ82

and the general direction of the solution. As with the team communication, every customer and stakeholder communication opportunity is a chance to get feedback and improve your understanding. Your future guesses and assumptions will be better and closer to the mark.

Successful Product Owners communicate with the team instinctively and continuously – and with the stakeholders and customers regularly and effectively.

The problem is, the team is right there. But the stakeholders and the customers are usually not as easily available. The only way to succeed is to have a very concrete and conscious approach to keeping constant stakeholder and customer contact. Sometimes, this means that you must (gasp!) leave the office!

There are five things you should do:

1. Be in regular contact with your own customer "best friends." Call them or visit them at least monthly if you don't have other information exchange.
2. Talk to marketing and product management on how customers outside your immediate contact list could be engaged for feedback. You could use webinars or key customer off-site events to gather feedback.
3. Regular email "newsletter" to all stakeholders.
4. Regular demo sessions.
5. Walk around the office unofficially and talk to people.

Communicating with your own customer contacts should happen regularly. Most of the time, these contacts are high-volume business for your company anyway. They also usually are fast to try any new features you release. As such, they'll probably have frequent insight and feedback on the new features, and even questions on how far they can push the technology. You must take this opportunity to help them and to listen to their thoughts. And while you have their attention, you should, when possible and appropriate, ask their opinion and feedback on your current ongoing items. Most people are eager to offer their opinions. In more complex scenarios, invite them to visit the R&D facility and give them a one-on-one demo.

You should work together with product management and marketing on webinars or key customer events. They can be very effective in getting feedback from one or several customers, but, of course, they take more effort to arrange.

We already talked about the newsletter in the routines chapter. The newsletter should be kept short, preferably image-rich (screenshots from new features, for example) and you should aim for it to be a fast read. The main thing is to call for action – invite feedback – and get people to ask questions and give comments. You know you've succeeded when people are reading the newsletter and you're getting questions about the contents.

The demo sessions are invaluable as a communication tool. A successful demo session:

- Demonstrates real end user features and focuses on the benefits that end users have from the new features,

- Is recorded for those people who couldn't attend,
- Isn't too long (30-45 minutes maximum),
- Is happening regularly,
- Is popular, so that you get all the important stakeholders to participate or view the recording,
- Succeeds in giving you feedback on the new features and other product requirements.

Finally, the value of just dropping by people's office and having an unofficial chat about anything, should not be underestimated. You can have something on your mind and go to the salesperson's room and just ask if they have a minute, and then ask them a question about something. They're usually happy to answer to you. But the real value of this kind of unplanned chats is that they're very likely to ask you something in return. They might have something on their mind about the next release, or they've just heard a related question from a customer. By walking into their office, you're giving them an easy opportunity to ask you a question.

Prerelease Often

We'll talk more about releasing later, but releases that go out of the door in one way or another are the key to get pilot customers or trial customers to use the new features. Sometimes, you might feel that the product isn't ready

Feedback from good enough is better than trying to delight users with perfection.

to be shown, but this early feedback is invaluable. You either confirm your assumptions or you redirect your development efforts. In the latter case, the earlier such redirection can be made, the better. Getting feedback from "good enough" is much better than trying to perfect something without the feedback! Of course, sometimes doing releases too frequently might irritate some of your customers! You need to find a good balance.

Pilot use can, and should, happen in stages. As the solution is developed from requirements and user needs toward the final, releasable product, the pilot customer could help the team and product owner in all stages by:

- Discussing the user problem and user needs,
- Reviewing initial prototype user interface,
- Trying out first functional prototype version in the R&D lab,
- Trying out prerelease version in the R&D lab,
- Installing the prerelease version to trial use at customer premises,
- Installing the prerelease to production use at customer premises, and/or
- Installing the final release version to production use.

Doing the development this way, in stages, is much more likely to result in a good solution that's easy to sell, buy, install, learn, and use. You shouldn't try to build a perfect solution in the dark chambers of R&D to be released upon an unsuspecting world – this is guaranteed to fail. Successful products are always built iteratively. Naturally, if the solution needs to be kept secret, you can have pilot users sign nondisclosure agreements.

Avoid Pilot Customer Bias

Having pilot customers takes time. There can only be a limited number of them. How do you avoid developing a system just for their needs? There are a few ways to approach this problem.

First, you should try to get representative pilot customers who are different from each other. If one is large, the other should be smaller. If one has expert users, you should try to have another who has users who aren't so well trained or knowledgeable. You should try to span the user capabilities and needs with the different pilot customers, not have them all from the same mold.

You could also target a certain customer group with each release. This way, even if you have quite similar pilot or reference customers, you're gearing this specific release for their needs. Next, the release could be targeted toward a different target customer group. This way, while you have a tight focus on any one release, over time, your product will be useful for many different customer groups.

Third, you should try to screen the pilot customer feedback through your own market knowledge filter. If a pilot user starts to request things that seem to be specific to her only, you can certainly listen to all her suggestions, but try to think whether these issues are minor or irrelevant for other customer types. Your task as Product Owner in these pilot user feedback discussions is to identify the critical and major things to change in the product before release. Maintaining such market knowledge is your responsibility as Product Owner, and it will generally require that you have contact directly with multiple different types of customers and end users – or if such contact is difficult, then, at least, you can talk to and interview people in your organization who have such contact opportunities.

Finally, one thing that will assist you is a clear product and release vision. When you get feedback about some feature, making a choice whether it's a critical or noncritical is easier when you can reference it against the product vision. Remember, you don't have to do the categorization by yourself. You can enlist the help of Product Managers, usability experts, sales, marketing, and development team members.

The Wheel of Success and Principle #2

You must be in frequent communication with customers. You must use information you gain from this to constantly iterate the content on what the teams are doing, the priorities, and the product vision. The vision, current state, and direction must be communicated constantly to the team. You must actively listen to your team members and encourage them. This way, you're sure to deliver a release that has the best possible value for the organization.

Summary – the Five Key Points

1. Regular interaction with the team and stakeholders is essential for success.
2. Communication and feedback from those close to you comes naturally, but you must work harder the farther away the stakeholders are.
3. Give encouragement and feedback to the team.
4. Activate everyone to think. Listen to what your team is telling you.
5. Make sure you have representative pilot customers, and that you engage them to give you feedback as early and as often as possible and convenient.

Principle #3:
Optimal Ownership

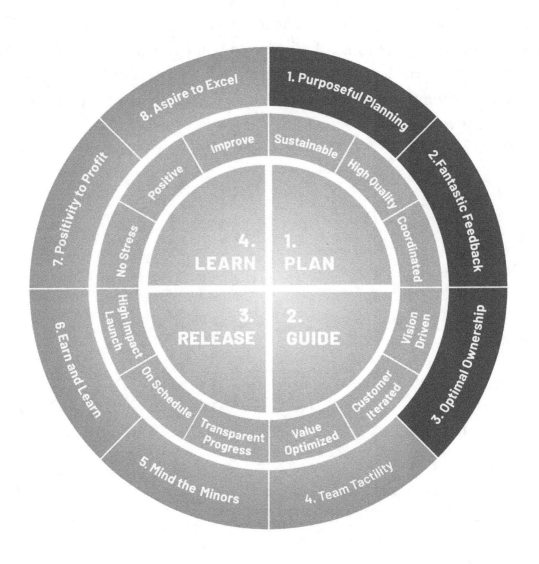

WHAT IT MEANS:

The role you're in is called *Product Owner.* When you own some-thing, you care for it. *Optimal ownership* means that you act as if the product is yours. You own it. You care for it. You know it intimately. You know why it exists and what problems it's meant to solve. You know where it's going and how it will grow.

But you also understand the big picture – as much as it feels like the product you own is your baby, it's not a person. It's only a product. It exists to solve customer problems, and, more often than not, products have a lifecycle. You also understand that your product isn't the highest priority of the organization.

BEWARE:

The Product Owner should be aware of following risks:

- Making decisions solely from the point of view of the product – forgetting the big picture.
- Not delegating enough.
- Not having enough stakeholder communication or customer insight.
- Not admitting to making wrong decisions.

Be Decisive

You should familiarize yourself with the features and aspects of the product, the customers and their problems, and the customer environment. You should know your product intimately. This allows you to be confident when there is a need for a decision. One of the key responsibilities in being a Product Owner is making decisions from small decisions that need to be made every day to big decisions that only come up once a year. The important thing is that you're there to make them without fear. With intimate knowledge on the product and the customers, most of your decisions will be right. When you inevitably make a wrong decision, don't be afraid to admit it. When in doubt, make decisions fast, but be sensitive to test the decisions as soon as possible.

Don't fear to step on somebody's toes and don't shy away from your responsibility to drive the product toward your vision. Owners also think long term. They don't allow the product to degrade due to hasty or poor-quality work.

Of course, organizations are different. Some organizations allow much decision freedom for individual Product Owners. In other cases, someone else will make the big decisions. Product Owners, however, must think that it's their responsibility to drive the organization to make those important decisions. The development team must not stay idle and waiting for decisions. This is what *optimal ownership* means. The Product Owner must know what's optimal for her organization.

The larger the organization, the more the responsibility of the individual becomes vague. In larger companies, it's natural that the area of responsibility feels smaller. You tend to start to think that you exist in a small, tightly corralled space. Many times, the office space, company policies and rules, and communication style of the management enforce the feeling that you're just a small cog in the large machine, with little influence. Feeling like this can lead to inefficient decision making. If the Product Owner thinks that every decision must be made in a committee, it slows down the progress of the team.

One risk with active decision making and seeing yourself as the owner who must make decisions is that it's easy to fall into the role of "I make all the decisions." This will mean that you start to be in the controller role, making all the calls. This leads to a two mistakes mentioned in the common mistakes section: an inefficient way of working and a very busy Product Owner.

It would be better to try to delegate as much as possible. Any smaller decisions that can be made by someone else should be made by someone else. But the delegation must be active: you must tell the person that she is free to decide, you must make sure she knows the decision "limits" or boundaries, and you must make sure she knows how to communicate what she has decided.

When you make a lot of decisions, you inevitably make a wrong decision. You shouldn't be afraid to admit that a decision was wrong. Whenever such a situation occurs, it's a place to learn. Why did you make the wrong choice? How soon did you realize it? What could have led you to choosing the right choice the first time? How could you have tested the decision faster? Especially, when the decision is big or "irreversible," you should keep more options open and decide later. In most cases, though, a fast decision (with a proper follow-up to see whether it was the right one) is more productive.

If the reader is interested, a thought-provoking book on the subject of decisiveness and taking ownership of one's actions is *Extreme Ownership*[17] by Jocko Willink and Leif Babin. The reader should be aware that the book is set in a military setting, describing U.S. Navy Seal training and operations. Not everything from a military viewpoint can be applied to normal business, but certain key thoughts and concepts from the book can be valuable for the reader.

Keep Up Solution Health

Just as communicating enough to customers or remote team members or stakeholders needs conscious actions from the Product Owner, the long-term technical solution health needs some thinking. The Product Owner and the team architecture lead need to balance architectural work with new feature development. The pressure to deliver new features is usually very high. It's easy to forget to maintain the product or solution health.

The vision of where the product is going should guide larger architectural activities. This is another reason why product management and the Product Owner must maintain a vision for the product. The Product Owner and technology experts and architects or lead developers must

17 https://www.amazon.com/Extreme-Ownership-U-S-Navy-SEALs/dp/B015TM0RM4/

understand what bigger changes must be done for the product to be able to fulfill its intended role.

However, not everything needs to be done in large "architectural work" type of activities. Every time a new feature or function is being developed, the development team should also review the code around the new feature. Is it easy to implement the new feature? If it's not easy, why not? What could be changed in the structure of the code to make it easy to implement the new feature? Is the code easy to understand? How could we make it easy to read and understand?

It's far easier to refactor the code this way, in small chunks as new features are being developed, because you don't need to justify spending a week, a month, or two months refactoring something with no visible return. Having a refactoring mindset built into the development process itself will ease the pressure to do large architectural redesigns. It won't completely remove the need to do architecture work, but it will diminish it significantly.

As a Product Owner, you must make sure that the development team leans toward refactoring the code in a modular fashion, rather than allowing technical debt to accumulate and make working on the code slower and slower and more error prone over time. However, sometimes, products are nearing their end of life. In this kind of situation, the Product Owner must then balance more toward a "quick fix" rather than refactor something that's not going to live for much longer.

As Product Owner, when investigating how to implement a feature, you must make sure that you get the honest view of the developers on the need for refactoring or maintenance work around the feature that you requested. If you fail to do this, it's fairly likely that you're growing the refactoring debt, and life will begin to get slowly more painful over the coming years.

Know the Big Picture

To be able to make decisions, and to make sure that enough maintenance work is being done, you need to understand the big picture. You have to understand customer problems and requirements. Without regular communication to all stakeholders, you risk making wrong decisions. This will lead to you being timid in the decision making, which will, in turn, lead to the team stalling often while "somebody" makes the decision. Spending enough time talking to stakeholders, product management and customers will ensure you have a solid understanding of the big picture, and it will allow you to act with confidence.

> *Knowing the big picture allows you to confidently and openly make bold decisions.*

As important as making the decisions is, you must also be bold when communicating your decisions to others. Your decisions should never remain hidden. Actively telling what has been decided allows others to learn what is going on and offers a chance for feedback. This kind of behavior also builds trust, allowing you to continue to make decisions actively, and even increasing your sphere of influence in the organization.

Understanding the big picture means that you can't think of only your product all the time. Companies usually have more than one product, and this leads to situations where different products are competing for the available development resources. Rather than blindly believing that your product should get the resources, you should work with others to understand what is the optimum use of the resources for the whole organization.

Importance of the Vision

A product vision should define what the product is promising to the end users, what problems it solves and how it differs from the competition. The following is a good guideline on product vision definition:

- Who is going to buy the product? Who is the target customer?
- Which customer needs will the product address?
- Which product attributes are critical for satisfying the needs selected, and, therefore, the success of the product?
- How does the product compare against existing products, both from competitors and the same company? What are the product's unique selling points?
- What is the target timeframe and budget to develop and launch the product?

Answering the questions above will help the Product Owner understand the target user, and her needs. The understanding on what features are most important will help prioritize and maybe even prune the feature set.

The vision will allow the Product Owner to have a concrete basis on which to do the prioritization decisions. It also will allow her to communicate the vision to the development teams, allowing them to understand the decision logic and what's important and what's not. In the long run, if the development teams understand the vision, they're able to use it themselves to make small design choices and increasing their level of self-organization. They can do decisions themselves when they know the vision and direction to which the product should be going.

A Fresh Vision Allows Optimal Ownership

Too often, the product vision is missing, outdated or overlooked. Even when somebody has created it, it was done years ago, and not kept up-to-date. The product vision should be kept up front and center, preferably on the development team room wall. It should be kept up-to-date.

Every year, every quarter, and even every release that goes out to customers is an opportunity to check if the vision needs to be adjusted. Every major product release probably has certain key features that take center stage. It would be odd if major new releases wouldn't affect the product vision in some small way. At the least, the product management and Product Owner can discuss and confirm how the major new features fit into the product vision.

The vision can also be useful when you must negotiate with the stakeholders on priorities, and when you have to say "no" to something. Rejecting an idea is much easier when you evaluate it against what the product is targeting to do. For the least amount of waste, ideas should be rejected actively and as soon as possible, preferably before they load the development team in any way. An updated and solid vision assists and enables this. It allows you to continuously reflect if something should be done or not against the product mission. When you inevitably make someone irritated or frustrated by rejecting her idea, you have a solid ground because you can refer to the vision.

The vision should not only be shared with the development team, it's also essential that it's communicated actively to the stakeholders of the product. People buy into the vision easier if they're involved in its creation, so it might be a good idea to involve sales, marketing, and company management in updating the vision.

Vision and Clear Goals Empower a Self-Organized Team

Fresh vision and detailed goals that are based on it are very important in enabling self-organized teams. The one thing that makes a self-organized team possible is that each team member knows what the team is trying to accomplish. When executed well, self-organization can yield higher motivation, faster and more correct reactions, and more and better ideas and creativity.

However, getting a team to be self-organized is a lot of work. Changing how people think takes time and effort. If everyone in the team is used to a more top-down management approach, getting them to take initiative is a huge task and requires months and possibly even years of conscious work. The reward of all this work is a highly motivated, fast, agile, and robust team that will outperform a traditional manager-led non-self-organized team any day of the week.

A good book on this topic is *Turn the Ship Around*[18] by David Marquet. It describes how important vision, goals, communication, and training are in transforming a team to be more self-organized.

Common Vision Spurs Targeted Innovation

A common vision also focuses the brainpower in the whole organization to target innovations related to the vision. Rather than have the ideas stream freely, the vision can be used to target any innovative efforts. If any new idea matches the release or product vision, it can be an interesting one to investigate further. Whenever the idea doesn't seem to match to the vision, the Product Owner can redirect the creativity of the individual toward areas that would match better.

Release vision also allows easier control of feature creep. More than that, it allows the team to target their thoughts and innovation power specifically to areas that definitely are interesting and potentially valuable for the release.

---

18   https://www.amazon.com/Turn-Ship-Around-Building-Breaking-ebook/dp/B015QQ10HE/

The Wheel of Success and Principle #3

The Optimal ownership principle means taking charge, ensuring that decisions are being made, impediments are being removed, and the product is moving ahead. In all the decisiveness, it must be remembered that every action that you as the Product Owner make is guided by a vision.

That same vision should be kept up-to-date and communicated to everybody else in the organization and especially development teams. Optimal ownership also means that you can delegate decisions to others, and everybody can act, guided by the same vision.

Without a common vision, such delegation becomes very difficult, the teams will become confused, and you'll have to resort to "central control." This will make you as the Product Owner very busy and the likelihood of success will drop.

Summary – the Five Key Points

1. Act decisively – be bold in making decisions.
2. Base your decisiveness on a clear product vision and good market knowledge. Maintain both actively.
3. Communicate not only your decisions but also the vision actively to everyone.
4. Use the shared vision to delegate tasks and decisions to reduce the team's dependency on you.
5. Think beyond the immediate future and make sure that the product isn't building technical or refactoring debt.

Principle #4: Team Tactility

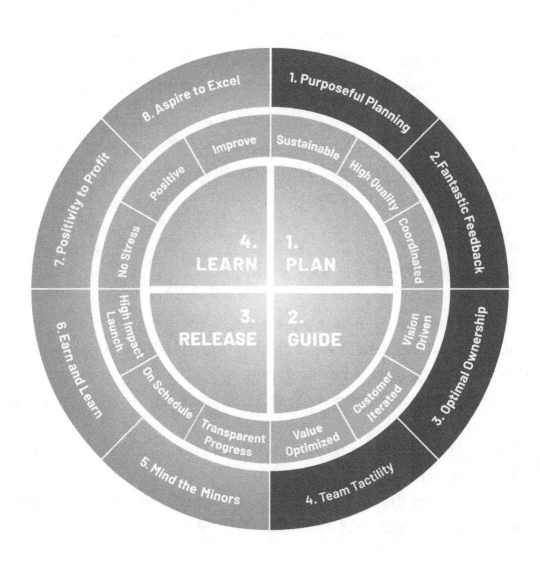

WHAT IT MEANS:

You cannot succeed if you're not available. A successful Product Owner practices *Team Tactility* – is located close to the team, in the same room or the room next door. In addition to the location, also the mindset of being present and available is important. You have to be open to people, available for questions, and when you do get a question, focus on the person asking, and listen to her. If you don't get enough questions, walk around and ask them yourself.

BEWARE:

The Product Owner should be aware of the following risks:

- Being too busy to focus on people.
- Not listening to what people are saying.
- Hoarding all decisions – not delegating enough.

Same Room – Same Boat

Although there has been debate and studies about software developers and open offices versus having their own rooms, there is a definite benefit of having the whole team share a large room, the R&D chamber.

Communication and information sharing are always one of the biggest challenges. Whenever any team talks about what they should improve, or what will guarantee success, one thing is almost guaranteed to surface: good communication.

Humans have evolved to work well in small groups, and we have usually a built-in desire to work in teams of three to eight persons. In larger teams, the teamwork gets a bit more inefficient. A team of eight or fewer persons is, in most cases, possible to fit into a single large team office. Why get everyone to the same room,

A common R&D chamber makes communication efficient – but make sure that you have good common room rules to enable some privacy!

even at the expense of having to sit really close to each other? The information sharing that you get in the room is priceless. People hear discussions and it's very easy to ask questions or advice. Stand up meetings are easy to arrange and people are never late because they're already there. Team room walls can contain task lists, designs, or vision definition.

There are some drawbacks to the one common team room approach; mainly the lack of privacy, space, and peace and quiet. Most of these are possible to remedy with some common agreements such as not having loud discussions or long meetings in the common room and using signals such as wearing headphones for "do not disturb."

The Product Owner should also sit in the common room. The main benefits with the Product Owner sitting in the same room as the team are:

- It will make it very easy for team members to come and ask questions.
- The Product Owner can overhear developer-to-developer discussions.
- Identifying when a team overextends itself is easy.
- It will make the team feel that the Product Owner is part of the team.

Ease of Asking Questions

It's important that the protocol for asking questions is as informal as possible. The greatest informality is achieved when developers can just shout and invite the Product Owner over to visit them at their desk. This is easy when everybody is in the same room. This also means that the room shouldn't be filled with people, making it difficult to walk to each other's desks.

Overhearing Discussions

Even though the discussions should be done in low voice in order not to disturb others, a curious Product Owner can hear when two developers are talking about something. Or, she can hear if they're not discussing something that they perhaps should be talking about. There should be a healthy amount of talk regarding design choices within the team. Even though peer reviews and pair programming are development team internal affairs, managed by the team, and coached by the Scrum Master, it doesn't hurt that the Product Owner knows what's going on.

One thing that should also happen is that when the team members move tasks from one person to another, for example from a developer to a tester, there should optimally be some form of handover chat. Moving backlog items just by assigning to the next person in an electronic tool such as JIRA, risks the handover information sharing being less than optimal. It's always better for developers and testers to have a short chat when handing over a task from implementation to testing.

Identifying Overloading

One problem that's especially common with teams that have good team spirit and high motivation to achieve the common target, is that they try to do too much. This can lead to the team constantly overloading the sprint – taking on too much work at the same time. If the team is using Kanban instead of Scrum, the overeager team can stop obeying the work-in-progress limits and have too many items ongoing.

The Product Owner who's close to the team should watch if this happens and step in. Starting too many tasks and not being able to finish them leads inevitably to more task switching. Task switching leads to poor quality and an increased level of stress. It's far better to keep the team close to the proven team capacity. The velocity should be the true indicator on how much to start. The work-in-progress limits should be followed closely.

Signal That You're in the Same Boat

It's important that the team feels that the Product Owner is part of the team. This further reduces any barriers for asking questions and makes team spirit better. It's difficult to maintain this feeling if the Product Owner is sitting far away from the team.

Sometimes, sitting in the same room is difficult due to space constraints. The next best thing is to have a room next door, immediately next to the R&D chamber.

Not Possible to Be in the Same Room?

It isn't always possible to be physically near the team. This could be because the implementation team is in a different building or city or even country. Quite often, the project also includes a subcontracted team or individuals who are off-site.

The target should always be to have the development team co-located, meaning that any subcontractors are located with the rest of the developers at the company offices. Having everyone at the same site, and same room is extremely valuable. It will speed up communication and ensure that the right product is built. The number of bugs, problems, and conflicts is reduced, and any troubleshooting is much faster than when the team is spread out to different locations.

When the Product Owner cannot be sitting with the team, then she should make a similar kind of conscious effort as with customer and stakeholder communication to visit as often as possible and use virtual presence tools such as chat tools or team room

Being in the same room will maximize the Product Owner's situational awareness!

tools to make it seem that she's as available as if she were sitting with the team. The physical distance cannot be an excuse for reducing the communication or allowing higher contact barriers to appear.

Whole Team Is Subcontracted

This is a very challenging but, unfortunately, quite common project setup; the company has decided to outsource a significant part of the R&D. On the company side, there is only one person – the Product Owner. The rest of the team is subcontracted and sits elsewhere. The reasons behind this sort of setup are usually the inability hire suitable talents or that the customer company decides that the R&D required in this project isn't their core competence.

The product ownership should always remain at the company control. However, if the Product Owner cannot sit with the implementation team, this presents a problem. How can you achieve all the co-location benefits described in this chapter? You can tackle this in two basic ways. First, the implementation team could appoint a person to act as an "engineering product owner" or "technical product owner." This could be the development team's Scrum Master, but it could also be a different person. This approach can work if the person on the development team has enough experience on the topic area to also do small decisions or "guesses" that quite often prove right. It should be emphasized that this kind of "second product owner" approach is always going to be more inefficient and riskier than having the true Product Owner close to the team. It adds another layer of ownership that's not benefiting the team or the project. Special care should be taken to have a good relationship between the Product Owner and the team lead in this case.

Another, perhaps better approach for the problem is to aggressively encourage use of virtual presence tools. Video conferencing, chat tools or team collaboration tools like Slack or Microsoft Teams. If there cannot be a Product Owner on site, she must make everyone feel as if she were.

Here are some rules for when the Product Owner cannot be on site:

- Visit the development team regularly, at least weekly.
- Have discussions with individual team members to build rapport and reduce their barrier to asking you direct questions.
- Encourage free and low-barrier use of chat or team collaboration tools to ask questions.
- Push for daily status checks, participate in the daily scrum via voice or video.

Video Is Worth a Thousand Words

Videoconferencing is the best substitute for co-location. The value added compared to just a voice conference is high, being able to see the other parties speeds up the meeting and builds trust and allows for more natural team dynamics to appear. Successful teams that aren't co-located use video conferencing actively.

Product Owner – Part of the Team or Not?

There are two schools of thought on the Product Owner being part of the team. One view is that the Product Owner isn't part of the team, and, in Scrum terms, is a chicken (from the classic scrum cartoon[19] of chicken and pig opening a restaurant). The other view is that Product Owners are as committed as the rest of the team to the deliverables of the team and is a team member (a pig). In the latter school of thought, the Product Owner participates as a normal team member to the scrum ceremonies.

If the Product Owner also works as a team member, one thing that must be remembered is that the Product Owner also has the role of approving the deliverable. If she is working on the deliverable, she also has to be able to take a step back and ask, is this good enough? Can I accept this? But this is exactly what any *owner* of something would do. For example, if you're repairing your own car or working on your own house, or have somebody else working on your car, you most certainly are thinking all the time when the repair work is being done – is this good enough quality for me? If you, at some point, get a sensation that the guys helping you repair your car are cutting corners and doing too hurried a job, you should stop them and say something. That's exactly what the Product Owner should be doing in agile development.

19 https://en.wikipedia.org/wiki/The_Chicken_and_the_Pig

Participating in Meetings

As part of the development team, the Product Owner should participate in all the development team meetings: daily stand up, retrospectives, sprint demo and review, backlog grooming, and sprint planning. Especially for backlog grooming and sprint planning, the Product Owner also must prepare quite well, presenting her proposal for the next sprint and planning what the grooming session should handle this week.

Occasionally there are also other types of meetings that the Product Owner must attend. For example, release planning or user story writing workshops. Anything that has to do with multiple backlog items or what gets released is the Product Owner's responsibility. Other types of meetings to participate in are individual story-related meetings that handle usability or user experience. If there are meetings on technical implementation or detailed design, these could be optional for the Product Owner.

Encouraging Questions

Depending on the persons in the team or the culture that you're working with, people have different levels of barrier for asking questions. You should be sensitive to the situation and try to find out how high individual barriers for asking questions are. Sometimes, your team members are coming from an organizational or cultural background that makes them very hesitant to contact you and ask questions. Sometimes, the individuals are just happier to work by themselves and don't ask questions unless prompted. You as the Product Owner must identify this situation and then do whatever you can to encourage communication to a level that you're happy with.

Agile methodologies describe ceremonies where the discussion about the implemented items is supposed to happen, but it's quite often easy to forget that the discussion doesn't need to stop there. The agile manifesto[20] itself encourages communication, stating that interaction and collaboration is more important than processes, tools, documentation, or following a plan. Don't hide behind Scrum! Discussion also needs to happen outside the Scrum ceremonies!

Even after the work has started, the discussion shouldn't stop. *Small discussions* that happen during the implementation is a new ceremony that the Product Owner and the team members can take into use.

The Small Discussions – Ceremony

As soon as you know that a developer has started on an item that you find interesting (and what isn't interesting? – they're working on a product that you own!) you allow them some time to get familiar and get started on the task, and then, if they're not coming to you to ask questions, you go to them and ask how it's going. You just want to check up if they're happy, what they've learned, and if they now know something new about the task that they didn't know before.

20 http://agilemanifesto.org/

Without exception, the developer has a far better understanding of the task after working on it for a while. If the task's estimated duration is, for example, 3 days (3 × 6 hours = 18 effective hours), you could jump in after a few hours and ask if they have uncovered something that's difficult, or if there are

The Small Discussions ceremony is one of the best secret ways for achieving extra team performance!

unclear items in the description. Often, both of these have been found. Rather than allowing the developer to dwell on the difficulties for hours or days, and resist coming to you with questions, you should reduce the threshold by walking to them and asking how it's going.

The small discussions ceremony is one of the best secret formulas for extra team performance. First, by going to them and asking, you're showing that you're curious, interested, and care about the end result. It makes them feel like they're working on an important task. Second, you get a chance to guide the result to a direction that feels right. You should listen to their concerns and guide them, if they have already made some progress with the implementation.

Third, the quality will be better, because it's almost inevitable that you can make the specification better at this point or add details to the list of acceptance criteria. If needed, invite a tester over and talk about how the item will be tested. When developers know how a story will be tested, they usually make sure that the tests pass before they say it's ready for handover.

Doing small discussions is easy when you're in the same room, and it becomes progressively more difficult if you're further away. Being on a different floor is the same as if you were in a different city. Successful Product Owners are simply located with the team. But, more than that, they walk around and are curious.

The Wheel of Success and Principle #4

The Product Owner must remain close and available to the team. This allows her to feel the pulse of the team and to control that the team doesn't overload itself. In addition, the availability will allow the Product Owner to constantly help, support, and guide the team toward the correct goal. By being embedded with the team, the Product Owner's situational awareness is at a maximum. At any given time, she can instantly give a complete, truthful, and transparent situation review to anyone who's interested.

Summary – the Five Key Points

1. Sit with the team in the same room, or the room next door.
2. Participate in the Scrum meetings.
3. Open door – always ask policy.
4. Focus on people and listen to them.
5. Walk around and ask questions – be curious.

Principle #5:
Mind the Minors

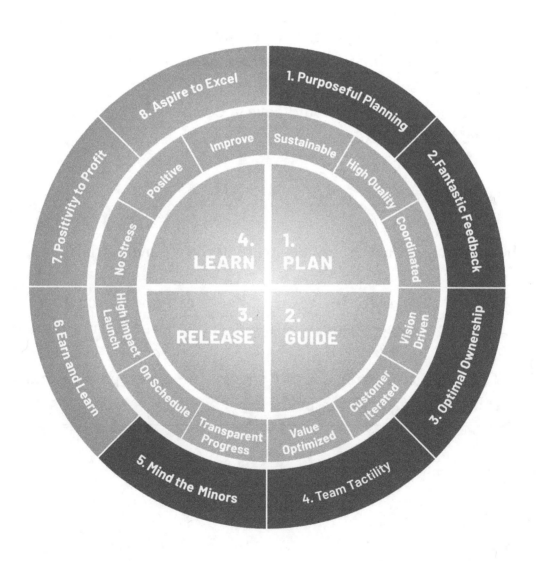

WHAT IT MEANS:

The Product Owner should constantly be *Minding the Minors*, observing that the team members are focusing on the highest priority work from the backlog. She should define and agree with the team what are the prioritization criteria for stories and severity classes for bugs. Clear rules on what severity bugs should be fixed at what stage should be established. The Product Owner should participate in the error screening process or meeting or do the error screening herself. More severe errors should be fixed as high priority work, but the Product Owner should have good control over when minor or trivial bugs are fixed.

BEWARE:

The Product Owner should be aware of the following risks:

- Left to their own devices, engineers can spend considerable amount of time in sugarcoating or fixing issues that are minor or trivial.
- The Product Owner doesn't engage the developers to understand true impact of issues.

Fixing Minors Is Low-Priority Work

One constant danger that the Product Owner must be aware of is that it's fairly easy for the team to get too bogged down on minor details, feature creep, or low-priority bugs. Constant vigilance must be kept on implementing only what's needed and avoiding sugarcoating new implementation. On the error front, it's, of course, necessary to fix errors and keep the error count low. However, the Product Owner should control when the team spends effort on fixing minor errors.

Minor issues come in two flavors – when looking at bugs, they come in the form of minor and trivial bugs. Minor bugs can often be categorized as very small visual errors or functional errors that aren't irritating or embarrassing, and aren't even noticed by most of the end users. Trivial bugs are even less severe as minor bugs. One has to remember that if a bug seems to be categorized as minor and it's then found to be irritating to somebody, then it's not a minor error but a major error.

The organization should establish rules for what kind of quality level is the target for the product. Some products may require a very low bug count at the time of release, in which case, it could be decided that also minor errors are higher than new feature development in the backlog. In other cases, more emphasis might be put on new feature development, and some number of minor bugs are permitted to exist in the product.

Fix minor errors in an economical way – in camps, using cheaper resources or while doing other work to the root-cause component.

Of course, a very low open bug count is the target for any organization and any product, but, sometimes, fixing low priority bugs doesn't make business sense. The Product Owner should find out what makes the most sense and provides the most value for the organization, and then coordinate the fixing by positioning the minor bugs correctly in the team backlog.

One approach for minor errors could be that, once in a while, the team spends a week in an error-fixing mode and fixes as many errors as possible, including minors and trivial errors. With this approach, care should be taken not to increase the risk of regression errors too much. It could also be possible to assign the fixing of some minor errors to a lower-cost developer resource, if the team has access to such.

While it's always a good target to fix all errors that are found, it's very rarely possible or economical. Errors always exist, and they're constantly found and fixed. The Product Owner's job is to find the correct balance between what to fix and what not to fix, and when the product is good enough to be released.

A mature team focuses efforts to have a solid architecture in the product as well as a good code review and testing approach with high coverage of automatic tests, so that once features are released to production, they're of good quality and the amount of functional or regression errors that are found later on after release is very low.

Prioritization Guide

High priority

Low priority

FATAL ERRORS

CRITICAL ERRORS

MAJOR ERRORS

NEW USER STORIES

MINOR ERRORS

Figure 18 Typical prioritization guide

Fatal Errors

At the top of the priority list are fatal errors (sometimes, also known as "showstoppers"). These are typically things that have to be fixed immediately – the presence of the fatal error is costing a lot every second it exists. These can be build breaks, unmanaged interface changes, significant functional area errors, and so on. In some cases, if a fatal problem is reported from the field, a critical patch is needed urgently for released features.

A fatal error, when reported, must be investigated and fixed immediately. The Product Owner and the team must react quickly, preferably within minutes of noticing the issue. Work on other backlog items stops immediately and the most suitable person is assigned to the investigation. Communication about the state of the error must be very active.

Critical Errors

Critical errors are significant functional errors. The error is easy to reproduce and prevents use of some core feature of the product. End users are certain to notice and get irritated by this kind of error. The product cannot usually contain any critical errors at time of release. Sometimes, a visual error is a critical one, if it's too noticeable or embarrassing.

Critical errors are always at the top of the backlog. They can be assigned to developers or in the sprint backlog, but unlike fatal errors, discovery of a new critical error doesn't stop already ongoing work. The assigned person starts work on the critical error after she finishes working on her current task.

Major Errors

Major errors are functional errors or significant visual errors that could potentially remain in a released product. They may occur rarely, or have extremely easy workarounds for the end users, so that the irritation level is low enough, allowing them to be major rather than critical.

The team and organization can set a rule on the number of major errors allowed to exist in a production release. On the backlog, major errors must be of higher priority than new feature implementation; otherwise, the number of errors would inevitably rise.

Minor Errors

Minor errors are typically visual errors or such extremely small functional errors that the end users aren't likely to notice or even understand to be errors. Minor errors could be prioritized below the new user story implementation because usually it's more urgent to get the new features in the backlog implemented to the point that they can be demoed or put into production.

Fixing the minors could be also done with "bug fixing camps" or "bug fixing weeks" that aim to fix, review and verify as many errors as possible. Additionally, in the same manner as software refactoring, it makes sense to fix minor errors, if something else is implemented to the component that's the likely source of the minor error.

The exception to this is when new features are being developed. The target should be that the feature is completely implemented, tested, and all the bugs that will be fixed are fixed, including minor bugs. This way, there shouldn't be a high number of unfixed minor bugs later when the features are released.

The team could also have a rule that if the effort to fix an error is lower than, say, 15 minutes (including testing) then it can be fixed without placing it into the backlog, if the regression risk from the fix is very low.

The motivation for keeping a tight control on fixing of minors is that the business value of fixing the minors is quite low compared to other items on the backlog.

Trivial Errors

Even less important than minors, the default action for a trivial error should be to reject it.

Error Screening

How can the Product Owner "mind the minors," control that the team is working on fatal, critical, and major errors, and then the user stories – and avoid the team spending too much effort on minor errors? To achieve this, the Product Owner must make sure that the severity is correctly set for all errors and monitor the work to see if someone is working on a minor error.

If the Product Owner is clear in her communication with the team, the team knows that they shouldn't work on minors without her approval. In this case, the most common way to work on a minor is to report as major or critical when, in fact it isn't so severe. That's why reviewing the error inflow is important.

There are two ways to do this in the inflow review: a constant error screening by the Product Owner or trusted "Error Manager," or a screening meeting at regular intervals.

The screening meeting is usually hosted by the Product Owner, Error Manager, or Test Lead and invitees can include the lead developers and the Scrum Master. The meeting looks at the inflow of errors and checks that the quality of the error is good enough. Ideally, it would be beneficial if someone has attempted to reproduce the error based on the error description before the screening meeting. Reproduction will give a confirmation for the screening team that the error is valid, and the steps in the description are correct. Then the error can be approved for work or assigned to a developer.

Testing the reproducibility is important because, quite often, the developers aren't experts in error reproduction, and the first comment from their mouths is "it works on my computer." So, it's far more efficient if someone from the team (usually a person with testing competence) attempts to reproduce the error before assigning it to a developer. If the tester isn't able to reproduce it, she can try different kinds of approaches, test environments and test steps to try to reproduce it, and if there seems to be any ambiguity in the reported test steps, further information can be requested from the error originator.

The Importance of When the Error Isn't Reproduced

A good quality error was already described in Table 3 earlier. The Product Owner should coach the team to produce all the information and log it to the error description. Often overlooked but very important is information about situations when the error isn't reproduced such as:

- If an error is always reproduced in a certain environment, but with the exact same steps, it's not reproduced in another environment.

- If the error is always reproduced with certain test steps, but with slightly different test steps it's never reproduced.
- If the error is always reproduced with certain release, but never in any other.

This will start to give the person who investigates the root cause a good idea where to look and speeds up resolution.

When the error has all this information and is known to be reproducible, then the Product Owner or the error screening team can easily make sure that the severity is also correct. And when the severity is correct, it's easy to avoid spending effort on minor or trivial issues.

Sugarcoating

It can be a natural tendency for the team to try to make the "best" implementation. Sometimes, especially when the Product Owner isn't available for the team to comment on ongoing work, the developers might spend their time and effort on making a feature unnecessarily fancy, beautiful, or complex.

The best way to avoid this is to be available and check on how the implementation is progressing. The Product Owner could review unfinished work and redirect it so that she's happy that the quality is good enough. Remember: It's better to release good enough and get feedback from customers rather than try to perfect something without feedback.

When the team is estimating the effort for a story, sometimes it can be that the work was actually easier than the team originally thought. If the Product Owner isn't around to ask and check, it could happen that the developer chooses to spend the estimated effort anyway, as she "got permission" to spend that effort for this backlog item. This could be stopped if the Product Owner was checking up on her and finds that the implementation is already good enough.

The Wheel of Success and Principle #5

Product Owners must develop an instinct for prioritization. The team must be constantly working on things that are most important, and the backlog must be kept ready with the next most important things for them to start working on. The priorities tie into the coordination as well – all the teams and people in the organization must know what's important and what isn't important. With shared awareness of priorities, there are less conflicts, and people pull in the same direction.

Summary – the Five Key Points

1. Establish an error screening process.
2. Define clear rules for priority of work.
3. Supervise the team to avoid hidden sugarcoating.
4. Postpone work on minor errors.
5. Avoid increasing technical debt[21] by engaging the team to understand if the team is doing enough refactoring.

21   https://en.wikipedia.org/wiki/Technical_debt

Principle #6:
Earn and Learn

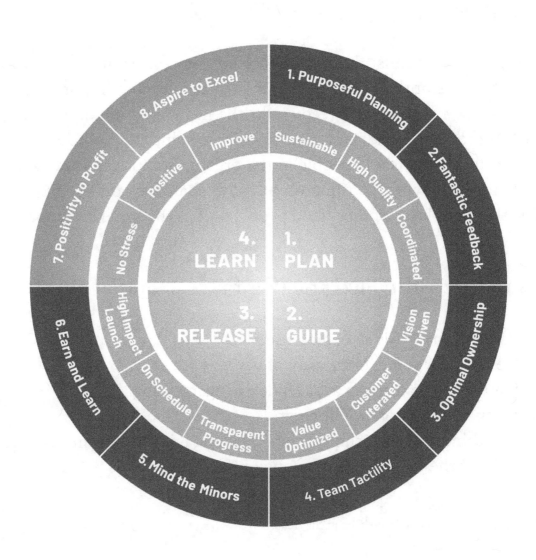

WHAT IT MEANS:

Making a successful release should be the main target for the team. Successful teams release frequently to *Earn and Learn* as much as they can. Releasing is the most important way to get value from the work that was done. The Product Owner should have two basic instincts: instinct for priorities, and instinct for release scope. The Product Owner should also actively work with other parts of the organization, marketing, sales, product management, customer support, and operations to make all the components of a successful release click together.

BEWARE:

The Product Owner should be aware of the following risks:

- Allowing feature creep – the release scope increases and pushes the schedule further and further.
- Not being able to use release vision to limit what's included in the release.
- Forgetting to think about other activities, especially marketing and thinking how to get users interested to start to use the new release.

Release Is the Only Way to Start Gaining Value

You can have the best team, the best backlog, the best Continuous Integration environment, the best customer insight, the best implementation, and best quality, but all of it is totally meaningless if you don't *release* your product. Your product must get into the hands of people who will use it, provide feedback, and allow you to adjust your course, priorities, and keep moving ahead.

Regular releases are like pins in a map, they show you exactly where you are. The development work between the releases is based on everyone's best guess what should be done. The success of a release is an undisputed marker on how well the work on the development of the features was done.

Release success isn't only dependent on the quality of the solution that was developed. A release that nobody knows anything about, or that gets no users, is worthless. How will your customers know about the release? What are the benefits of the solution or the new features developed in this release? What incentives do they have to upgrade? How easy is it for them to purchase or upgrade? What is the trigger that will make them decide? How good is your release sales pitch?

The analysis and decision on what is the "lure" that will get people to buy or upgrade to the release is more the responsibility of product management. Of course, you as the Product Owner will work with them on defining it and implementing the necessary things to make it happen.

Sensible Scope

The Product Owner is the person who has the responsibility of the backlog, and she usually also has much to say on the details of what gets implemented or fixed in any release. The product management outlines larger feature or EPIC level decisions on what each release contains, but the Product Owner manages the detail level work. The product and release vision should act as a guide on what to include and what to postpone.

The Product Owner is in the perfect position to fine-tune the release contents to be such as to provide maximum value for the organization. The value can be monetary, business, or customer value, or it can be knowledge value, increasing understanding of the market or customer needs or decreasing uncertainty on critical assumptions.

There will always be more and more fixes, features and changes that people want to push to be part of the next release. The Product Owner is the person who needs to make the decision to include them or not. If the Product Owner keeps just saying yes, yes, we'll fix this, we'll change this, we'll include this – the release will be significantly postponed, or

The Product vision defines the product in 5 years' time. The Release vision defines the product after the next release. The Release vision can be used to group features together to support each other and the release marketing message.

it will never get out. So, the main thing the Product Owner needs to learn is to say "no," choose the correct things to be included, and postpone the rest.

As Fatal and Critical level errors are always naturally fixed for the next release, the focus for the Product Owner lies in major and minor errors and new features and change requests. It's exactly here that having a release vision will help the Product Owner in the decision making.

A release vision defines what this release of the product will do better than previous releases. Since it will be used as the basis for a marketing story – the reason why customers should purchase this release or upgrade to this release – the release vision must guide what gets selected into the release on the individual bug and feature level.

Let's take an example. Suppose the release vision is *"Increased ease of installation and initial setup of the product."* This will be first analyzed and split into EPICs and stories and then the development team will

> *Release without a vision is a maintenance release!*

implement the stories and verify them. Let's then say that during the verification and in the final testing, from the demos or from the field, some bugs are found that are related to initial setup or ease of installation. Normally, and in the past, these kinds of bugs may have been categorized as major or even minor. But now, they're exactly matching the release vision! Fixing them now makes a lot of sense. They might have been small irritations in the past, but when the release is now attempting to market itself as "installation friendly," there can't be even the smallest blemish on that message! The release vision helps to choose which major or minor errors are selected to be fixed in the release.

Let's take another example. Suppose no release specific vision is defined. The backlog contains backlog items and EPICs in priority order, but the release is chosen to contain "just the most important things" from the top of the backlog. There is no common denominator between the stories. What is the release vision now? If one can be defined, it's surely much vaguer than in our previous example. How will it help in choosing which errors to fix and which not? It won't help in that. Nor will it be very effective as a basis for a marketing message. A release without a clear, single-minded vision very easily becomes a maintenance release that won't effectively sway customers to purchase or upgrade.

Minimum Viable Product (MVP) Negotiations

Most readers of this book will probably come from environments in which the products under development are either all software, or have considerable amount of software components in them. An inconvenient truth about software development is that there's a lot more uncertainty than in other types of products. The increased level of uncertainty means that almost invariably, while the team targets to develop a specific set of features in an agreed time, it usually encounters unforeseen problems and has some trouble delivering the original targeted feature set. What does this mean? It means that some features will get delayed, and that means, that the persons who were interested in exactly those features are going to be slightly irritated.

This situation can lead to conflicts inside the organization. A good Product Owner manages this situation by regularly and transparently communicating the status and the plan to all stakeholders, and also emphasizing the priority order and the reasoning behind the prioritization. It's much easier to understand why one's favorite feature is delayed if you see and realize what features were deemed more important and why. This creates a sense of being in the same boat.

The higher the product's release frequency is, the less of a problem this is. If you're doing release once a year, missing one release deadline will be a huge problem. If you're doing releases once a month, it might be a small problem but people will be much calmer. If you're doing releases weekly or daily, they're not even going to notice.

In some environments (for example in highly regulated industries with long official product tests and validation processes), doing releases very frequently isn't easy, and the need for transparency in status and prioritization is all the more important. In these situations, the Product Owner must also become quite skilled in forecasting and managing the likely scope of the release. In essence, she'll be thinking about the Minimum Viable Product in the original definition of the term: what feature set is getting the organization the most return on investment with an acceptable level of schedule risk. Of course, all of this will also need to take into consideration the development team's spirit and level of stress. Can they stretch and include something? Would doing so result in taking risks in quality or increased technical debt? Managing the scope of the release is the responsibility of the Product Owner and doing so successfully requires keeping a constant eye on the team's velocity, release burndown, and the estimated clarity on the backlog.

If the release cycle is long, and the team has initially targeted too large set of features and is then forced to "rescope" the release, this inevitably erodes organizational goodwill toward the team and the Product Owner. There are only so many times the Product Owner can tell the stakeholders that the development work has to be rescoped. Doing it once is usually okay. The second time is sure to raise some eyebrows. Three or more times and the stakeholders are starting to question the Product Owner's competence.

Hopefully the reader will see the benefits of doing releases frequently. With frequent releases, the backlog doesn't have to be estimated so far into the future to generate an accurate release burndown, and the risk of missing a single release deadline doesn't create high levels of conflict in the organization.

Always Ready to Release

Making a successful release is a result of managing the scope, but it's also a result of maintaining a high level of quality throughout the development. Doing quality work is more the responsibility of the team itself, but the Product Owner can be of assistance.

Develop in Vertical Slices

When developing larger features or EPICs, the Product Owner is participating in the splitting of the EPIC or large story into smaller stories. One thing that's important in the story splitting is that each story ends up delivering some end-to-end testable functionality. A larger feature should be developed in vertical slices so that even after the delivery of the initial slice, a small part of the final solution is testable end-to-end. Subsequent stories expand the initial small end-to-end functionality until the final story delivers the final piece of the puzzle.

The alternative to this, delivering nonvertical platforms that stack up, eventually delivering all the features to the end user, will seem easier initially, but it's guaranteed to result in a huge number of integration and functional errors when the final story is delivered, because real meaningful testing can be started only after the final story.

Integrate All the Time

Again, more an issue for the team to take care of, but the Product Owner can also try to remember to emphasize the importance of integrating everyone's code all the time (typically, at least once a day). Doing this will reduce integration issues later.

The alternative to constant integration, or Continuous Integration, is to work on individual development branches. Some special situations could force the team to use a development branch, but a general rule is that the team should use a common development code branch and maintain this branch to near production quality level throughout the development.

Other Things to Assist in Reducing the Maturation Period

Other activities that the team should use effectively are:

- Continuous Integration with test automation.
- Testing each story to production level tests after story is implemented and not relying on "release testing."
- Continuously think if the Definition of Done is still accurate and valid.

Is Marketing on Board?

Having built the best features won't help if nobody knows about it, and if you have not thought about what will incentivize the customers to make the purchase decision. The purchase trigger must be a consideration throughout the development work since it can impact the feature selection of the release, or even the specifications. Sales, product management and marketing must be involved in defining the "why" for the release. This is very closely related to the release vision.

If the upgrade or purchase trigger has been defined, there still remains the work of planning the marketing communications. Marketing will need assistance in this. The Product Owner can typically give demos and prepare presentations for marketing that outline the benefits of the total release and the individual features in the release. It's much better that the benefits are listed by the Product Owner and then marketing interprets them to "marketing speak."

This all takes time. Marketing probably doesn't know or realize when it should start to prepare the story, so the Product Owner having the ownership of the schedule should remember to coordinate with marketing on these activities.

Support the Customer Support

One final thing that can fail the successful release is if the customer support is unprepared. If the actual release is good, marketing succeeds and the customers swarm to make the purchase, but if customer support isn't briefed and doesn't know how to help customers who have problems, then the whole release will be hurt.

Involving customer support is difficult because they're typically always busy. It's difficult to get time and bandwidth for them to comment on or review features under development. Here, the Product Owner must use her imagination on how to get them to learn the new features.

A combination of:

- Good documentation on new features,
- Manuals,
- Helper tools,
- Demo sessions,
- Training sessions,
- Getting customer support involved in final release testing, and
- Pilot customer use

are good activities that ensure that customer support is prepared for the product release.

The Wheel of Success and Principle #6

Releasing the team's work successfully is the only way to start gaining benefits back to the organization. Successful releasing means frequent, on-schedule, high-quality releases that are well coordinated with other functions in the company. Keeping the schedule means actively managing the release scope and ensuring that team delivers production level quality all the time and the maturation period at the end is as short as possible.

Summary – the Five Key Points

1. Don't fear to make the release.
2. Base release scope decisions on product and release vision.
3. Keep constant control on release scope and actively postpone everything that's not critical for the current release.
4. Have an integrated, end-to-end visibility of the solution maturity to avoid long maturation time after code complete.
5. Support other parts of the organization in planning for successful release.

Principle #7:
Positivity to Profit

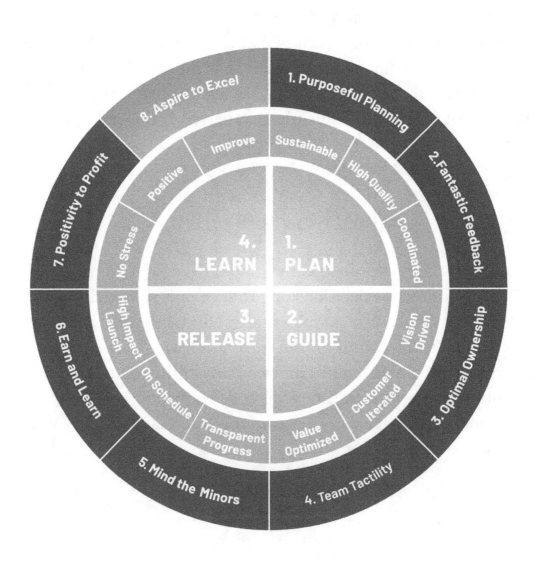

WHAT IT MEANS:

People are the most important resource for any organization. The employees are unique. Everybody can use money, technology, or have a fancy office location. But nobody else has the same people. Happy people are more efficient, achieve better results and are more creative. *Positivity leads to Profit.*

As the Product Owner is responsible for maximizing the team's results, performance, and the product development speed, she must also make sure that the team is feeling positive and happy. A positive person and a positive team produce more profit.

BEWARE:

The Product Owner should be aware of the following risks:

- Only focusing on issues and backlog items and forgetting to focus on people and their well-being.
- Forgetting to thank people and celebrate successes.
- Forgetting to encourage people to have positive breaks during the day.
- Forgetting to ensure a happy state of mind during times when creativity is needed.
- Forgetting how important team building is for new teams.
- Forgetting to reap the benefits of team happiness – not challenging the team or the people enough.

Work Should Be Fun

Every team member should feel every morning that it's fun to come to work. The work should be challenging and meaningful. Your colleagues should be odd, interesting, and fun. If your colleagues seem normal, you just don't know them well enough!

Teams should spend time together to have fun, to develop a common spirit, and to care about one another.

In any given project, there will be countless situations where an individual won't be able to tackle the issue at hand without help. Team members are much more likely and willing to help when they know each other and can trust each other. Even more importantly, people are more likely to ask for help when there is trust in the team. Being able to trust each other is a function of achieving results together, but it's also about having the feeling of being in the same boat, feeling of camaraderie.

Positive team spirit needs to be constantly nursed to remain on a good level. Of course, this isn't only the Product Owner's job, but she must ensure that the team is feeling good. A happy team is more productive. Once the team starts to understand that it's allowed to have fun, and they're allowed to have short breaks, tell jokes, and several times a day do something that makes them feel good, they start to show initiative themselves to remain happy and find fun ways to get to know each other better.

You can do several things to get the team feeling better:

- Candy and sweets in the meeting room (or fruit, if you're a health nut!),
- Lunch time together,
- Meetings outside in the sun and nature (even a "walking meeting"),
- Team building events,
- Dinner together,
- Games in the team break room,
- Encourage people to have enough breaks and do something they enjoy during the break,
- See the funny side of things and laugh at yourself,

Taking breaks shouldn't be seen as something "forbidden." Short breaks, especially if one does something that results in a happy state of mind, increase productivity. The happy state of mind is key here. During these breaks, one should avoid watching anything negative, such as news or the status of your investment portfolio. Rather, spend the time listening to uplifting music, watching cat videos on YouTube, or playing a game. Whatever increases your energy.

Of course, the breaks shouldn't be too long. Extended breaks start to irritate the management.

Be a Builder of Teams

An absolutely essential thing to remember is that a new team or one with a lot of new members requires more focus on team building and getting to know people than a mature team. This seems self-evident; however, new and growing teams are always very busy and have challenging schedules, so it can feel difficult to set aside time for team-building activities.

If your colleagues don't seem odd, you just don't know them well enough!

Team building is an investment that builds trust and speeds things up. A couple of hours or even a day spent outside the office in getting to know who you're working with definitely will result in speedier implementation when the team gets back to work.

Happiness Multiplies Creativity

Product development needs creativity. Creativity is much stronger when the person is happy. A positively thinking brain is able to see opportunities and is much more likely to grasp those opportunities than a neutral or a negatively thinking brain. When a person is in a positive mood, she doesn't fear failure as much. This leads to increased courage and boldness in taking actions and making decisions.

An excellent resource on the reasons why positive thinking affects creativity is the book *Happiness Advantage*[22] by Shawn Achor. This book will help you understand that the happy brain is more effective, and positive thinking leads to more success.

22 https://www.amazon.com/Happiness-Advantage-Principles-Psychology-Performance/dp/0307591549

Positivity also supports teamwork. When people in the team know each other, the level of trust is increased. When the team members are in a good mood, they're much more inclined to help and support others. Delegation of decision making is more efficient when the individuals are able to creatively see opportunities and have the courage to make the decision themselves. In this way, investing in keeping the team feeling good actually speeds things up. People will be more proactive and more likely to take their own initiative and act without being told to or instructed. This helps in reducing the Product Owner's workload and results in more efficient use of the team's brain power.

Power of Thank You

When did you last thank someone at work? In the last hour? Today? Yesterday? Last week? You don't remember? You, as the Product Owner, are in the position to approve the team deliverables. Therefore, you're also in the position to offer thanks to the people who helped in the product creation. People *expect* you to thank them if they do a good job. How will they feel if you forget to thank them?

Giving a clear thank you message is valuable in two ways. First, it's a small reward to the person who helped you and will generate feelings of happiness when given sincerely. Second, by showing gratitude, you're forced to consider what things are worth a lot to you. What things take you toward your target? By thinking and noticing the things that are valuable and worth thanking people for, you'll be more aware of them, and you can highlight these accomplishments when you're communicating to others.

Thanking people generates positive feelings not only in the person who gave the thank you and the person who received it. When used actively and intelligently, thanking people can reveal small achievements that will also make everyone feel that the team is making valuable progress!

A good habit for Product Owners is to thank one person each day. Try it out; you'll be surprised how easily you'll learn to see new positive things around you. You can also coach the team to be more appreciative of other team members' work, further increasing the amount of positive feedback in the team.

Stress Leads to Waste

Stress directly and strongly reduces creativity. This is a result of evolution. Over hundreds of thousands of years we've been living in a dangerous world, full of predators. The fear of being eaten is still within us. A threat or a dangerous situation will revive those old mechanisms deep in the human brain. When threatened, we tend to focus on action, not thinking creatively, because in millions of encounters with the sharp teeth of a predator, pausing to think creatively has gotten us killed. In stressful

Regularly thanking people teaches you to identify valuable achievements which can be communicated widely, generating an increased feeling of success in the whole team.

situations, evolution has taught us that it's better to run, and run fast. Preferably, climb a tree.

Another possible reaction in stressful situations is to fight. Never mind who is right; if you feel stressed, you typically have an enemy nearby. The brain starts to think of ways to defeat the enemy. We're unlikely to think creatively and listen to what other people are saying if we're very stressed.

On the other hand, it's possible to reduce this threat-effect by just allowing a stream of small positive moments to break the monotony of the office. These can be very personal, like listening to music, watching a funny video, or thinking about one's family. The positive moments can also be something that the team members do together. A game, a joke, a chat, or having lunch together. The de-stressing moments should happen many times a day to keep the brain primed with happy thoughts.

The Product Owner should be aware of the benefits of positive thinking to creativity, and she should be thinking how she can make sure that the development team is de-stressed regularly, especially when creativity is required, such as in design or planning meetings.

Meetings should start always with a mention of a recent good result or other type of team success, or by sharing of candy. In most individuals, sugar is a surprisingly powerful substance

> *Don't underestimate the power of sugar!*

that triggers feeling of happiness. Studies have shown that sugar significantly impacts knowledge workers' success in complex tasks. Even the mere thought of eating sugar works in same way.

Speak with a Smile

The importance of positive and encouraging communication style is huge. The Product Owner will need to speak and present quite often, and she is in front of people constantly. In addition to these more public presentations, she is talking to people one-on-one every day.

Given the importance of positive thinking, you can surely see that there's a huge potential in keeping all of these communication opportunities positive rather than negative. If the Product Owner remembers to keep a positive style in all her communication, it will make it much easier to get people to act creatively, help, support and assist the project activities.

Even seemingly bad news, like a failed test or a delayed activity can be given a positive spin: what did we learn from this? How can we improve? What do we now understand better? Do we now see more opportunity for action?

Losada-Ratio

Organizations have a critical positivity ratio[23] called Losada-ratio. Simplified, the ratio means that if the team communicates, for every negatively styled communication, there needs to be three or more positively styled communications. If the team is at this threshold, three

23   https://en.wikipedia.org/wiki/Critical_positivity_ratio

times more positive communication than negative, the team is doing all right. If the ratio is higher and there is, for example, five times more positive communication than negative, then the organization is in a positive spiral. The team will learn, grow, improve, and work much more efficiently. If there's too much negatively styled communication, for example, if the ratio is 1:1, then the team will work very inefficiently and find it very difficult to improve its ways of working.

Product Owners must coach their team and organization to communicate in a positive style. This will result in huge improvements in creativity, positivity, self-organization, willingness to support others, and team effectiveness.

The style of positive communication doesn't mean that failures or negative issues are forgotten, swept under the rug, or overlooked. On the contrary, they should get as much or even more focus than before because every failure is an excellent learning and improvement opportunity. But the style of reacting to these adversities must be positive, rather than negative.

Almost anything can be given a positive spin. For example, a serious error has surfaced. Excellent! Now we know about it! Can the error be reproduced easily? Wonderful! An error that's reproduced and surfaced can certainly be corrected. Imagine if we hadn't found this error now and we would have made a release. Now that would have been a disaster.

What to Avoid

There are two very dangerous things that the team and the Product Owner should learn to avoid. The first is *knockout communication*. Knockout communication means when someone makes a suggestion, then the instant reaction from others is try to find fault with the suggestion or say why it won't work. They're trying to knock the idea out, make it fall to the floor.

Think about this. How does the person who made the suggestion feel when every time she suggests something, it's immediately met with a hostile, fault-finding attitude? Why would she continue to make suggestions? Only masochists would do so.

Trying to find out why something is a bad idea is pretty instinctive behavior, and some people do it more than others. It's possible to learn from this, but the individuals who are doing it, must be coached out of this kind of behavior.

You want people to think independently and make suggestions. Maintaining a self-organized, self-guided team is also very difficult when there is instant criticism for any action or idea.

The second dangerous thing is a *cynical approach*. Cynical comments about the product, team, plan, ideas, or future are dangerous because they erode the trust and belief that the team can succeed. People who regularly display cynicism should be coached out of this and shown why a more constructive approach to offer their opinion would be much more valuable.

A successful team doesn't say bad things about others behind their backs. This is a form of cynicism and there should be an absolute zero tolerance for such behavior.

Bugs Are Gold Nuggets

Testing is like digging for gold. You're not sure, but you suspect there are some bugs (gold nuggets) hidden in the software under test. You just have to find them. When you find a nugget, it should be a moment of joy, right? You're

Test camp is a gold rush. Bugs are gold nuggets – find them and become rich!

richer than a moment ago! You have more information value right now because you know about the bug. If you know the details, the steps and environmental conditions how to repeat the bug, you're even richer, the gold nugget is bigger!

The best bugs are ones that have been discovered and are repeatable, because engineers can always fix a bug that has been identified, described in detail, and is repeatable.

When thinking about bugs, it's easy to see them as negative things. Things to be avoided. The problem is, bugs will always exist, because the creative work of product development isn't perfect. You don't start with perfect information on the problem or the customer need, and you have humans doing product development work. Humans make mistakes.

Some industries, of course, cannot afford to have lots of errors (aerospace, medical, nuclear, etc.). Thus, in these industries, a lot more activities exist to reduce the amount of errors to a minimum. It's much more common and much more economical to not see errors or bugs as negative things but just as facts of product development, and welcome them when they're discovered in a systematic and repeatable way.

Summary – the Five Key Points

1. Positive feeling and positive thoughts increase team performance and creativity.
2. Beware of situations that constantly overload the team or make the team stressed.
3. Team communication must remain in positive style.
4. Even problems or bugs must be seen in positive light.
5. Thank people daily, and coach others to do the same!

Principle #8:
Aspire to Excel

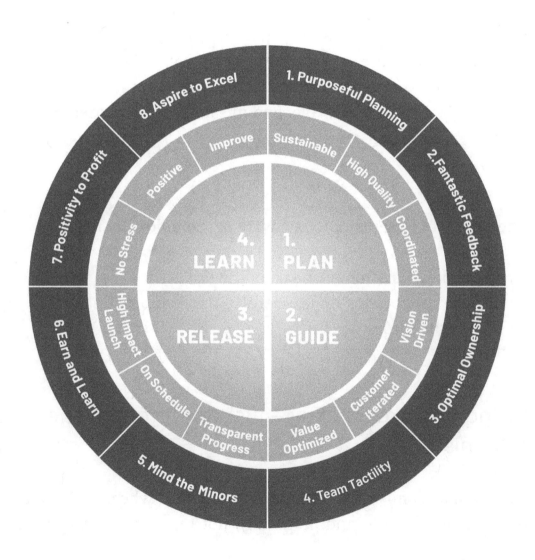

WHAT IT MEANS:

Everything that happens during the development work is a learning opportunity. Did you fail in something? Analyze why and try to avoid similar failures in the future. However, only learning from failures isn't enough. What do you want and need to do next, where do you want to be in the future? What are your current skills and capabilities and find out what you need to learn to succeed beyond the immediate future. You have to know what and where you want your product, your team, and yourself to be, and then you have to *Aspire to Excel* in the task, role, and mission you've chosen.

BEWARE:

The Product Owner should be aware of the following risks:

- Repeating the same mistakes in the project.
- Staying too focused on the here and now and not having goals set for the future.

Making mistakes is okay – just don't repeat the *same* mistakes

Everyone makes mistakes – the idea is to admit when you've made a mistake, learn from it, and, hopefully, not repeat the same mistakes over and over. This is true both for individuals and for the team. The team should learn to notice when the ways of working or the processes could be improved and then it should develop a habit of improvement. If the team fears making or admitting mistakes then its learning is much slower and it can be stuck in poor processes and be incapable of even thinking in a better way.

The successful Product Owner thinks about how the team can improve its ways of working, processes, and cooperation and remove any painful things in its environment. She also thinks about the individuals on the team and makes sure that they have a fruitful development path in the organization.

All this, looking at what's happening right now and finding ways to improve the current things, is geared toward keeping the team intact, positive, improving and, therefore, generating maximum results for the organization. Because the Product Owner wants the team to be able to deliver as much as possible, she must also be interested to ensuring that the team learns effectively.

On the other hand, Product Owners must not forget their own competence development. The role of Product Owner is an excellent view into the rest of the organization, but the Product Owner must have a vision and plan for herself. Where does she want to be 5 years from now? What skills and knowledge must she have? Don't forget to think about yourself. Most Product Owners tend to be less focused on themselves, and more focused on the product, the service, and the team. Don't forget to also learn actively yourself.

Good Retrospectives Are Essential

In Scrum, the team has retrospectives at the end of every sprint, and both the Product Owner and the Scrum Master should participate in the retrospective as normal team members. The Scrum Master usually facilitates the team retrospective.

The team retrospective tries to identify what works well (so they can continue doing it) and what isn't working so well (so it can be improved). Usually, it's a good idea to only select one or two things from each retrospective to improve, so that it would be certain that those things are actually improved before the next retrospective is held. Facilitating retrospectives is a skill that's easy to learn. You can find several methods online and in books[24] that will help you learn how to do it.

A team retrospective will usually highlight issues in the team's ways of working, but it will also often identify things in the rest of the organization that would need to be improved. One of the most common finding is poor cooperation or communication with other teams or other parts of the organization. Even though the Product Owner doesn't need to be the person who takes ownership of the issues that the other teams or organization needs to improve (it can very well also be the Scrum Master, or somebody from the development team), she usually has the best working relationships and rapport with the other stakeholders in the organization. Thus, she is well placed in taking issues to them.

---

24 https://www.amazon.com/Agile-Retrospectives-Making-Teams-Great/dp/0977616649

Grow from Adversity

The team can identify places where it failed to do something. This can be done in retrospectives, but it doesn't have to be limited to them. Suggestions and improvements can also be done outside the retrospective ceremony.

A good team (and a good Product Owner) always keeps an eye out for what was done, how it worked, and what could have worked better. The continuous improvement shouldn't be only limited to the retrospective sessions. A good team is really committed to the sprint goal, and when some approach to achieving the sprint goal proves unsuccessful, another approach is tried. This way, the team learns continuously. The retrospective is an important ceremony, and it should be used for also identifying the areas needing improvement, and how they could be improved. But at the same time, the retrospective could be used to cement what the team has learned during the previous sprint.

Spread Excellence

How do organizations become excellent? Does it happen instantly all over the company? Or, are good ways of working and good working practices identified somewhere in the organization, and then actively mentored and deployed elsewhere? Almost certainly the latter is the case.

You, as the Product Owner, and your team should maintain a desire to work intelligently and learn what kind of ways of working, routines, tools, and technologies work best in your environment. In addition to this, you must have a desire to show, mentor, and coach others in your organization to learn and take into use the practices and tools that you have developed or noticed to work very well. This way, the whole company or organization benefits, grows, and thrives.

What benefits will such a coaching approach offer for you and your team? First, the built-in desire to find out what works best in order to set example to others keeps pushing you onwards in your road to excellence. It forces you to learn even when you think you cannot. Second, by being in the front, setting the example, your and your team's sphere of influence will grow. Others will instinctively listen to you because you have repeatedly shown them improvements and given them useful tools that make work easier and more efficient. With this increased influence, your team has more power to effect change, and when more resources are needed, the selling of the investment idea to management is easier.

Where Do You Want to Go?

As we've seen, being a Product Owner is a busy role. If you learn to use the 8 Principles and the success factors presented in this book, you can use your time more effectively and engage the team to be more self-organized. This will save time and reduce the day-to-day pressure. But even so, the near-term target to deliver valuable releases is such a pervasive goal that it's easy to lose sight of what you want to achieve with your career long term.

As important as the product vision and release vision are for the development team, guiding them in analysis, design, implementation, and testing, and allowing you to prioritize work for them, equally important would be to maintain a personal vision of what you want to do in 5 years. Do you want to build your competence as a Product Owner, or do you want to pursue a career in program management, product management or line management? Do you want to learn how to sell and excel in sales?

You cannot effectively build your own skills and capabilities without first understanding where you want to be. As we've discussed in this book, in the same way as the product vision and release vision guide you in making the correct choices and priority setting, your own vision will guide you in learning the skills that prepare you for your future.

The Wheel of Success and Principle #8

What are you good at? What would you like to improve? What would you need to learn? Where do you want to be? When you understand these things, you can prioritize and seek what kind of practical actions are available to you to improve yourself.

Learning takes time, and you must be ruthless in finding the time from your schedule for your own personal improvement. Find out what you love to learn and go out and learn it!

Summary – The Five Key Points

1. Continuous team improvement from retrospectives.
2. Learn from adversities – don't repeat the same mistakes.
3. Be a seed for excellence in your organization.
4. Where do you want to be?
5. What is going to help you get there?

Summary

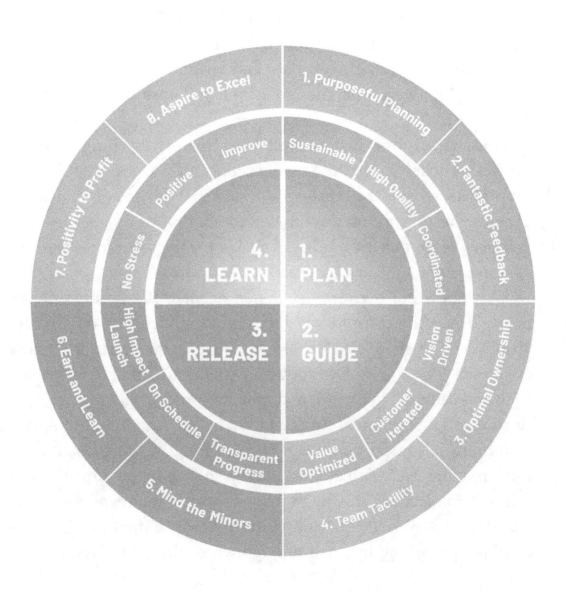

A Successful Product Owner:

1. **Plans with a purpose,** focusing on the near term, low uncertainty events, making sure that the next weeks and months have valuable work that's clear, understood, and high priority. The Product Owner cooperates with others on the long-term outlook

2. Seeks and provides **fantastic feedback**, using constant customer iterations to optimize the value of the team releases, and improving the team actively by coaching and giving feedback on the team performance. Everything the Product Owner does is done with high transparency.

3. **Minds the minors**, instinctively prioritizes everything based on market feedback so that the team is constantly aware what is highest priority, what is the release scope and spends time on things that generate best return on the time invested.

4. Practices **team tactility,** being available for the team for questions, steering, comments, and complaints.

5. Displays **optimal ownership**: When needed, the Product Owner boldly drives the team forward, basing every decision on a shared vision and actively delegating tasks to the self-organized and empowered team. The successful Product Owner is also able to take a step back and see the big picture and how her product fits in it.

6. **Earn and Learn:** Release frequently and on schedule, the release containing a logical and an easy-to-sell set of features that are implemented with high quality, and no showstopper surprises after release. You achieve this by making sure that the team works in a sustainable way, not overloading itself, produce high quality deliverables by working in small enough, vertically integrated backlog

items. The quality is kept near production level throughout the development, maintaining a constant release capability.

7. Understands that **positivity results in profit,** emphasizing low-stress, fun, and happiness as sources of creative solutions and sustainable delivery of high quality.

8. Makes sure that she individually and the team **aspire to improve** with a purpose, and spread their excellence to other parts of the organization

With the 8 Principles, the Product Owner Success Factors and the Wheel of Success, your success as a Product Owner and your future development to any role or position you desire is within your grasp.

Recommended Reading

Following books offer excellent insight and knowledge on issues that are valuable and important for any Product Owner and are highly recommended.

Book	Author	Comments
Inspired: How to Create Products Customers Love (ISBN 978-0981690407)	Marty Cagan	Excellent resource for Product Managers and Product Owners. Describes how successful tech companies consistently innovate and avoid waste. Book describes Product Manager as also taking the role of the Product Owner.
The Happiness Advantage (ISBN 978-0307591548)	Shawn Achor	Shows and proves the value of positive thoughts on creativity, innovativeness and success. This book will help the reader to understand why the team should not be overstressed and why creative solutions can only effectively surface when people are feeling good.

Book	Author	Comments
The New One Minute Manager (ISBN 978-0062367549)	Spencer Johnson	A delightfully short book, the main take-away from the book is the importance of giving feedback and acknowledging when the team or a person does a good job.
Turn the Ship Around (ISBN 978-1591846406)	David Marquet	A lesson on the difficulty but immense rewards of building a self-organized team.
Extreme Ownership (ISBN 978-1250183866)	Jocko Willink, Leif Babin	Highlights the importance of taking ownership and leadership.
Agile Retrospectives: Making Good Teams Great (ISBN 978-0977616640)	Esther Derby, Diana Larsen	Good resource for a beginner retrospective facilitator

Acknowledgements

The writing of this book was more work than I thought it would be. In fact, I think this project validates the age-old truth that you should always multiply your estimates by pi. Because I think that the effort of creating this book has been about 3.14159 times more than I anticipated.

I probably wouldn't have even started to write the book without Sylvia. I probably wouldn't have finished the book without support from Henri. And the comments from Tanja, Henri, and especially Petri have been instrumental in the book taking the present form that you now hold in your hands. Special thank you to Nadja[25] for the amazing graphics and images.

And finally – the real basis of what I have written here is my experience in working with so many nice and intelligent people over the years. My ex- or present colleague; should you now be reading this, working with you has been a pleasure, and this book is born in part from our voyage together.